FEMINIST SCHOLARS' EXPERIENCES IN DECOLONISING THE ACADEMY

Jan Etienne (Ed)

FEMINIST SCHOLARS' EXPERIENCES IN DECOLONISING THE ACADEMY

Race, Class, and Identity in Narrative

The Gender Studies Collection

Collection Editors

Jan Etienne & Reham ElMorally

LPp

Dedication: This book is dedicated to Linda, Ursula, and Gillian, and those other stalwart, decolonial feminist activist supporters who believe in global social justice and the struggle for a better social world.

First published in 2025 by Lived Places Publishing

British Library Cataloguing in Publication Data
A CIP record for this book is available from the British Library

ISBN: 9781915734082 (pbk)
ISBN: 9781915734105 (ePDF)
ISBN: 9781915734099 (ePUB)

The right of Jan Etienne to be identified as the Volume Editor of this work has been asserted by them in accordance with the Copyright, Design and Patents Act 1988.

Cover design by Fiachra McCarthy
Book design by Rachel Trolove of Twin Trail Design
Typeset by Newgen Publishing UK

Lived Places Publishing
Long Island
New York 11789

www.livedplacespublishing.com

Abstract

This book brings together the decolonising experiences of a diverse group of feminist scholars who demonstrate how perspectives on race, class, gender, social identity, sexuality, and disability impact lives and play a critical role in informing decolonising activism in higher education. The contributors explore the importance of (and the challenges they face, in) decolonising higher education in the modern-day neoliberal university.

Readership: Scholars and students interested in understanding the ways in which Black and decolonial feminist scholars are influencing decolonising programmes in the university sector.

Key words

Black feminist, Womanist, Decolonial feminist, Decolonising, Critical race theory, Intersectionality, Neoliberal, Social justice, Collaboration

Lead author's message

The book is written for scholars everywhere and is inspired by the work of feminist education activists at the sharp end of higher education campaigns for equality, justice, and inclusion.

The key aims of the book are:

- To encourage the development of Black and decolonial feminist approaches to help shape decolonising programmes in higher education.
- To promote practical understandings of Black Feminist Thought when using decolonial feminist approaches in higher education.

Contents

Acknowledgements

I would like to first express my deep appreciation to the hard-working, committed decolonial feminists, Black feminists and womanist contributors writing in this volume. I owe a debt of gratitude to members of the Womanism, Activism, Higher Education Research Network for your loyal support and energy, in reclaiming the decolonising narrative in higher education, using a Black feminist lens. Thank you to Linda Milbourne, Ursula Murray and Gillian Klein for your lifelong belief in fairness, justice and equality in all areas of higher education and for giving me a constructive, invaluable start in a journey to influence change.

Immense appreciation to Reham ElMorally, for your expertise, reliable support and careful proofreading of the final manuscript.

In particular, I extend much gratitude to Pauline Stephenson, Lloyd Gardner and Christina Howell-Richardson for observing intuitively from the sidelines and for reminding me of the reasons why collaborative work of this type matters. The struggle goes on and you guys certainly gave me food for thought. Most interestingly, your selected assertions and at times, measured silences kept me grounded.

Long may this unique Black feminist mission to decolonise the higher education Academy live on.

I thank our future readers and look forward to active discussion and engagement with the learning outcomes.

Finally, I thank David Parker and other colleagues at Lived Places Publishing for your patience and tireless support throughout the life of this project.

Jan Etienne (Ed)

About the contributors

Jan Etienne (Volume editor)

Dr Jan Etienne is a lecturer in Psychosocial Studies, in the Faculty of Humanities and Sciences at Birkbeck, University of London, UK, where she earned her PhD. Jan is chair of the Womanism, Activism, Higher Education Research Network, and a founding member of the Decolonising the Academy Collective. She is a graduate of the School for Policy Studies, University of Bristol, and author of *Communities of Activism: Black Women, Higher Education, and the Politics of Representation* (2020), and *Learning in Womanist Ways: Narratives of First-Generation African Caribbean Women* (2016).

Yasmin Adan

Yasmin Adan is an English teacher and social justice scholar. Her postgraduate research studies engage with the activism of Black female teachers using a Black feminist theoretical lens. She has an MSc in education, power and social change from Birkbeck and a BA in English literature from Queen Mary, University of London, UK.

Tanja Burkhard

Dr Tanja Burkhard is an assistant professor of qualitative methodologies in the College of Education & Human Development's Department of Educational Policy Studies at Georgia State University, Atlanta, USA. She earned her doctorate in Teaching & Learning at Ohio State University in 2017. Her research focuses on the deployment of critical qualitative methodologies to explore the intersections of racialisation, (im)migration, and gender in education. She is author of *Transnational Black Feminism and Qualitative Research: Black Women, Racialisation and Migration* (2022), and *Race, Justice and Activism in Literacy Instruction* (2023).

Nataliah Douglas

Nataliah Douglas is a teacher and head of the Faculty of Sociology and Social Sciences. Her research at Birkbeck, University of London, UK combines Black feminist and critical race theory approaches to explore the relationship between education, ethnicity, gender, and mental health. She has a BSc in sociology with honours and an MRes in social science research and psychosocial studies from the Department of Politics at Birkbeck, University of London, UK.

Sue Dunn

Dr Sue Dunn is a former associate lecturer in higher education. She has a PhD in biochemistry and taught and managed programmes for "non-traditional" adult students returning to study, with a particular focus on pedagogic practice for inclusion and diversity. She was appointed Director of Widening Participation at Queen Mary University, London, UK, and helped develop the master's programme in Education, Power, and Social Change at Birkbeck, University of London, UK.

Kerry Harman

Dr Kerry Harman is former director of the Research Centre for Social Change and Transformation in Higher Education at Birkbeck, University of London, UK. She led the MSc in Education and Social Justice in the School of Social Sciences. She is a founding member of the Decolonising the Academy Collective and the Feminist Imaginary Research Network, an international network of activist feminist artists, curators and educators in feminist galleries and libraries, and feminist adult educators.

Beverley Hayward

Dr Beverley Hayward is an associate lecturer in the Psychosocial Department at Birkbeck, University of London, UK. She teaches on the master's programme in Education and Social Justice. Having a learning disability and a working-class identity, she was often marginalised in the UK educational system. By exposing her vulnerabilities, she seeks to foster a transformative and democratic pedagogical student experience. She has a PhD in education, transformation and lifelong learning.

Nandita Sirker

Nandita Sirker is a doctoral student and associate lecturer at Birkbeck College University of London, UK. She graduated in 1984 with an LLB from the University of Warwick, UK, and came back into education after a 35-year career in statutory and voluntary sector children and family services. She is a trained mentor, early years leader and parenting facilitator. She gained an MSc in Education Power and Social Change from Birkbeck before commencing her PhD. She lives and works in London, UK, the city in which she was born. She has two adult children.

Joao Paulo Tinoco

Dr Joao Paulo Tinoco is a researcher with a PhD and a master's degree in linguistic studies from the Federal University of Mato Grosso do Sul (UFMS), Brazil. In 2022, he was awarded an overseas scholarship at Birkbeck, University of London, UK, funded by the PDSE/Capes Program. He also has a degree in English language and literature from the Federal University of Tocantins (UFT), Brazil.

Learning objectives

- Understand the role of decolonial feminism in decolonising agendas in higher education

- Understand the value and usefulness of Black feminist text in shaping decolonising initiatives

- Understand how to explore the role of identity and its usefulness in developing decolonising strategies

- Examine and widen understandings of how to promote, practical, inclusive learner support when designing decolonising programmes

- Critically assess and seek to understand ways of sharing decolonial feminist thinking with senior management

- Analyse and understand the relevance of Black feminist research in higher education decolonising programmes

- Explore understandings of decolonising strategies in meeting well- being needs

- Critically analyse own understandings of decolonial feminisms in the context of decolonising and the British higher education Academy.

- Analyse and understand the impact of responsibility for delivering equality (and diversity measures) on the Black female teacher

- Understand the nature of personal accountability in decolonising work in higher education

Introduction to chapters

Theme 1: Understanding Black and decolonial feminist perspectives in anti-racist, decolonising work in higher education

- In Chapter 1, Jan Etienne considers Black feminist and Black womanist practice in the context of lived experience – concrete experience as a criterion of meaning – and introduces us to the journey to uncover the usefulness of Black feminist thought (Collins, 2000). She discusses intersectionality and the nature of developing knowledge when the world was focused on the murder of George Floyd. Learning objective: Understand how far Black feminism can assist us in bringing feminist voices together to tackle institutional change and work towards decolonising higher education.

- In Chapter 2, Joao Tinoco explores the use of dialogue as a means of assessing knowledge claims and the value of using key text readings in decolonising work reflecting sexuality and "belonging". He discusses the Black feminist writings of Gloria Anzaldúa in Borderlands – La Frontera (Anzaldúa, 1989). Learning objective: Understand the value of Black feminist text in the higher education decolonising curriculum.

Theme 2: Sharing and using Black and decolonial feminist approaches in decolonising higher education

- In Chapter 3, Sue Dunn shares good practices in supporting student learning in higher education. She considers tutor identity and how Black feminist theory in the work of bell hooks (1999) has influenced her approaches and has helped her reflect on her own mixed heritage identity in the context of her "lived experience". How can discussions of tutor identity help raise learner and tutor confidence and at the same, meet decolonising goals in higher education? Learning objective: Understand how we build on widening participation and access programmes to develop decolonising activities in higher education.

- In Chapter 4, Beverley Hayward discusses White working-class identity and neurodiversity in approaches to Black feminist practices (hooks, 2002). She engages with an "ethic of care" and shares her arts-based teaching strategies where she promotes conversations that demonstrate the usefulness of Black feminism in decolonising programmes in higher education. Learning objective: Understand how visual arts-based approaches inspired by Black feminist thought, help demystify the decolonising programme in higher education.

Theme 3: Leading and delivering Black and decolonial feminist approaches in higher education

- In Chapter 5, Kerry Harman uses her own feminist imaginary approaches to connect with the work of Sara Ahmed (2023) and confronts the damages of neoliberalism in the British higher education academy. She employs a decolonial feminist perspective to explore "personal accountability and leadership in addressing neoliberal challenges within higher education". The focus is on fostering transformative change to advance decolonising practices and promote Equality, Diversity, and Inclusion. Learning objective: Examine strategies for encouraging senior management in higher education to integrate decolonial and Black feminist approaches into their daily practices, enhancing institutional EDI outcomes.

- In Chapter 6, Nandita Sirker addresses leadership lessons in Black feminist approaches and cites the work of the Combahee River Collective (1977) to demonstrate the uniqueness of Black feminism in inspiring change. In a chapter focused on "lived experience", she reflects on her research into mothering and refugee women and their access to services using the Black feminist lens of Gail Lewis and Audre Lorde. She combines critical race theory themes in an approach designed to amplify a leading role for Black feminist research in higher education. Learning objective: Understand the relationship between Black feminist research and the higher education decolonising programme.

- In Chapter 7, Jan Etienne, Yasmin Adan, and Nataliah Douglas consider an ethic of care and personal accountability in understandings of social justice (Lorde, 1989) and Black feminist activism in education. The chapter presents good practice in Black feminist thinking in decolonising programmes for social justice and well-being in higher education and demonstrates how adopting Black feminist approaches as outlined in the work of Black feminist Venus Evans-Winters (2019) and others can support good mental health and well-being in higher education. To what extent are Black female teachers carrying out decolonising work in addition to, or as part of their day-to-day duties? What lessons do they have for the higher education sector? Learning objective: Understand the nature of Black feminist approaches to an ethic of care and personal accountability in decolonising work in higher education.

- In the final chapter (8), Jan Etienne and Tanja Burkhard reflect on the global experiences of Black and decolonial feminist scholars in the context of UK higher education. The authors engage indirectly with the theme of "voice" and dialogue as a means of assessing knowledge claims in their own Black feminist qualitative studies, and refer to the work of other Black feminist scholars to highlight an understanding of an "ethic of care" in moving forward in anti-racist policy and practice in higher education. The contributors point to the works of Black British female academics, including voices such as those of Patricia Daley, Heidi Mirza, Avtar Brah, Anne Phoenix, Tracey Reynolds, and others. The need to demonstrate Black female leadership in decolonising UK higher education academies is paramount.

Theme one: Understanding Black and decolonial feminist approaches in anti-racist, decolonising work in higher education

Introduction

1

Thinking Black and decolonial feminist in higher education

A Black British womanist perspective

Jan Etienne

> What made Black women a powerful and legitimising force for mobilising both institutionally and nationally also made some of us unpopular in wider political arenas. (Mathibela, 2020, p. 134)

In the search for global social justice in higher education academies, this chapter addresses the urgency to deliver a Black feminist approach to the decolonising agenda. Today, Black and White feminist scholars can be said to be adopting a global approach to delivering change in contemporary decolonising cultural life, in a combined approach to sharing thinking and practice to further the decolonising agenda in higher education.

As Mathibela (2020) notes above, Black women are a powerful and legitimising force when mobilising. Nowhere can this be observed more starkly than in the higher education, decolonising institution. However, adopting a combined approach to a decolonising programme can also present challenging obstacles for those of us who feel it necessary to confront the absence of a nuanced Black feminist voice, one where the Black woman is not muted or diluted in a feminist frame. When we challenge this problem as womanist activists, we are considered Black feminist agitators and perceived as unpopular in a decolonising feminist frame, Black womanism challenges Black feminist approaches which continue to collude with White feminists' in marginalising the positions of Black Women. In such a feminist frame, decolonial feminism seeks to work with all feminist activists to dismantle colonial power structures and prioritise the voices, histories, and experiences of women from marginalised communities, particularly those affected by colonial legacies practice, one which has the ability to include a wide variety of perspectives from the lens of those impacted. In the context of our lived experience, (lived experience refers to the firsthand, everyday realities of individuals, particularly those from marginalised groups, which provide insight into broader systemic issues) we uncover the usefulness of Black feminist thought (Collins, 2000) and acknowledge its potential role in shaping strategies to promote equality, diversity and inclusion practices in higher education. In considering the valuable place of intersectionality (Crenshaw, 2003) in a UK setting, it has also been important for us to begin with some opening questions. First: Who hears the voice of the White working-class, female tutor, inspired by Black feminist theory and determined to decolonise approaches to social science teaching? Next: What can the Anglo-Asian, middle-class tutor tell us about her Black feminist-inspired practice, designed to mitigate the anxieties experienced by non-British research students attempting to navigate the structural barriers which stand in the way of their educational success?

In these current times of social conflict, conveyed via social media and impacting the lives of Black communities, it is necessary to give closer consideration to intersectionality (a framework that examines how different social identities, such as race, gender, and class, intersect and create overlapping systems of discrimination or privilege) and our various positionings in the ways in which we respond to emerging global social challenges. The "Summer of Racial Reckoning" (Burkhard, 2022) in the United States, and the nature of developing knowledges emerging when the world was focused on the murder of George Floyd, provided a collective impulse to renew our focus on decolonising work. Some of us concluded that such a major racial incident was indeed a catalyst for a new collaborative, decolonising project inside our UK university sector.

In this region, it became evident that higher education research centres in the United Kingdom were acknowledging the need to further publicly declare their intention to increase support for research on critical "race" studies, racialisation, and anti-racism. In pledging their commitment, British universities also declared their intention to amplify the research of Black scholars working on critical social theory, in particular. These institutions appear to be particularly keen to support interdisciplinary, innovative, and publicly engaged social research on issues that concern the impact of race discrimination and social inequalities on people's lives. However, what is the reality of such support, and what is the relationship with existing efforts to decolonise higher education? More importantly, to what extent are Black and decolonial feminist scholars in the British university inspired by such developments? The contributors to this volume have much to say about their own feminist approaches to Equality, Diversity and Inclusion (EDI) in higher education. In sharing their strategies, they are keen to foster mutual understandings of the ways in which collaborative efforts can emerge to achieve success in delivering effective decolonising programmes in higher education.

As authors, in this collaborative volume, there are similarities in our lived experience, and as a Black, womanist, feminist scholar, working alongside my colleagues, I commit to an appreciation of the key tenets of Black Feminist Thought (Collins, 2000) (a body of knowledge and practice developed by Black women that emphasises the importance of lived experiences, intersectionality, and resistance to systemic oppression), in particular, its approach to a collective decolonial feminist (Vergès, 2021) realism. In addition, while I acknowledge that a globalised, decolonial feminist framework aimed at delivering a decolonising agenda exists, I am mindful of the struggle to ensure our diverse voices are heard. In this regard, I ask: How do different gender identities interact and share knowledges in a challenging, decolonising higher education arena? We argue that Black feminist, womanist, and decolonial ways of thinking can influence change, and we highlight the practices in our day-to-day lives as diverse feminist scholars in a mission to transform the spaces of learning excellence in higher education.

In stories of hope for global social justice, we argue that a different approach to student support and engagement, focused largely on the principles of Black Feminist Thought (Collins, 2000) and new thinking in womanist and decolonial feminisms (Varges, 2021), is needed to strengthen approaches to decolonising the higher education academy.

Themes in the book

The narratives in this decolonising volume connect with critical dimensions of Black Feminist Thought across three themes as follows:

Each chapter in this book connects with a particular theme in the writings of key US- and British-based Black feminist theorists such as: Suraya Nazak, Patricia Hill Collins, bell hooks, Heidi Mirza, Alice Walker, Gloria Anzaldúa, Gail Lewis, Hortense Spillers, Sara Ahmed, and Audre Lorde. We argue that Black feminist theory can add a new dimension to understandings of personal, and collective responsibility for delivering unique change in decolonising strategies in today's diverse higher education institutions.

In recognising the need to address the missing and ignored voices, it is crucial that we revisit, reveal, and reassert Black feminisms and theorise intersectionality (Collins, 2019; Crenshaw, 1989; Nash, 2019) in respect to developing productive, decolonising practices. Not only are we seeking curriculum change involving intersectionality methodologies (Haynes et al., 2020), but practical changes in collective mindsets from those previously charged with single-handed responsibility for implementing change. In such ways, we allow for a recognition of our understanding of the multiple ways that discriminatory practices exist and the possibilities of responding to diverse social problems.

Black feminist thought (Collins, 2000) uniquely engages with Black feminist theory to create diversity and inclusion practices which deliver higher education decolonising strategies by utilising its key tenets of "lived experience", "personal accountability", "dialogue as a means of assessing knowledge claims", and an "ethic of care" (an approach that emphasises empathy, responsibility, and mutual respect in educational settings, fostering an environment where diverse identities are acknowledged and supported).

In such areas, it is possible to critically analyse the lived experiences of diverse groups of feminist scholars and draw on their pedagogical works to construct decolonising higher education programmes and approaches which expose the usefulness of Black feminist thinking.

Following the Summer of Racial Reckoning (Burkhard, 2022), such approaches have been uppermost in the minds of decolonial feminist proponents, who are determined to share ways of exposing Black feminist approaches as key and essential features of decolonising activities in higher education. As such, Black feminism is seen as a priority and can be observed in the wide adoption of Black feminist intersectionality (Crenshaw,1989) principles, designed to impact all sections of the university population, encouraging inclusive practices to be adopted. In this volume we argue that the adoption of Black feminist approaches is essential for improving well-being in higher education. What are some examples of such practices working in practice, and what are the issues preventing its liberal take-up in higher education institutions?

It is a problem that anti-racist scholars in the university at times have considered themselves unable (feel restricted) to put into practice measures which they believe, they are not fully able to articulate (Black feminist ways of thinking), as they perceive ownership of such priorities to belong elsewhere. Using a Black feminist lens is to think Black feminist and act in ways which prevent the prevalence of racial and sexual discrimination. And there are various ways that we can consider how our own experience of being oppressed can help us appreciate pressing concerns such as the relationship between mental well-being, race and gender. What is our active role in attending to the attainment gap (Choak, 2022), where Black students continue to lag behind their White counterparts?

Black feminist struggle is a struggle of the mainstream and as such, it calls for a collaborative mission to disrupt the processes which promote structural racism, sexism, and other forms of discrimination. The adoption of an intersectional, Black feminist approach to practices which include all higher education staff asks a key question: What is the nature of Black feminist thought in the decolonising agendas talked about inside the modern-day university? I argue that a response to such a question lies in Black feminist ways of reflexivity and must be treated with urgency. This involves creating spaces where staff work together, share the same room, and feel a collective energy for change. In an environment where discussing the prospect of change no longer feels bleak, we can move beyond mere discussions of 'mainstreaming' to focus on practical, actionable steps for transformation. Collaborative missions require reflexivity and a shared commitment to achieving meaningful change. Reflexivity fosters a deeper understanding of the issues raised by Black feminist commentators, but its practical application remains a critical question. In higher education, change-makers must rely on clear evidence to guide their efforts. This decolonising volume advocates for integrating the principles of Black feminist thought into contemporary teaching, research, and learning practices to drive transformative change

Why use Black feminist principles to decolonise higher education?

A first step to appreciating the usefulness of Black feminist theories in anti-racist decolonising work in higher education is to develop a strategic approach to identifying where it is used and practised. The use of Black feminist approaches, I argue, is more widespread than apparent. In raising the profile of Black feminist theory as an important prerequisite to delivering Diversity and Inclusion targets in higher education, it is important to discuss and focus on practical decolonising strategies developed by both Black and White decolonial higher education feminist scholars.

The appalling and high-profile murder of George Floyd in Minnesota, USA, in 2020, was a turning point in the thinking of anti-racists all over the world. Across the globe, we witnessed Black feminist educators and decolonial feminists in higher education coming together to search for justice for victims of institutional racism. However, neoliberal education policy and practice in higher education continue to threaten the enthusiasm, dedication, and ability of those committed to long-lasting remedies to dismantle structural inequality.

The surge in global support for the Black Lives Matter movement also spurred new interest from decolonial and Black feminist scholars to examine how their work (Jones, 2021) could be used to secure alternative ways of positioning the struggle for institutional change.

Intersectionality: Emerging out of Black feminist praxis

In discussions of intersectionality, for example, Crenshaw (1989), Collins (2019), Nash (2019), we are mindful of the Combahee Women's Collective's (1977) mantra: "If Black women were free, everyone else would be free since our freedom would necessitate the destruction of all other systems of oppression" (See Chapter 6, this volume). The book's overarching argument connects closely with ideas of intersectionality, in that Black feminist theory as a system of ideas and the diversity of Black feminist perspectives must first be understood to help us gain a wider appreciation of the impact of discrimination.

Intersectionality is explored in various chapters through the overlapping oppressions of class, disability, gender, and sexuality affecting both staff and learners, with a focus on enhancing understanding within the context of higher education. In analysing the works of Black feminist scholars Patricia Hill Collins, bell hooks, and others, we argue that when developing effective anti-racist decolonial strategies, sharing ideas and good practice is a priority. In these areas, we are encouraged to consider personal accountability, and to trust in our collaborations with others.

Black feminist engagement with womanist principles and the challenge of representation

Other approaches to Black feminism, including womanist principles, a term coined by Alice Walker (1983), acknowledge that feminism does not represent all Black women's experiences. Contemporary womanist thinking (Etienne, 2022) for some of us, is an awareness that Black feminism does not always represent our voice or state of being in the struggle for equality because of its total domination and preoccupation with the ideals of the White feminist. The language of Black womanism, I argue, represents a strategic framework for driving change (Etienne, 2016; Wahern, 2022), This approach rejects domination and calls for a new, enlightened, and anti-racist plan of action for fostering inclusion, particularly within research practices. and this calls for a non-acceptance of domination in a new, enlightened, anti-racist plan of action for inclusion, particularly in our research practice. At times in this volume, the terms Black feminist/womanist are used interchangeably (Chapter 6) to acknowledge that not all Black women identify as Black feminist. The work of Brown and Murray (2023), Lindsay-Dennis (2015), and Maparyan (2012) specifies womanism and womanist, not only in addressing the absence of Black women's voices in mainstream feminism but also look to prioritising community, using a distinct lens of care, reciprocity, resilience, and support, encouraging collaborative approaches to emerge when conducting anti-racist, decolonising work. In other areas, Black feminist essayist Hortense Spillers reminds us of the exclusion of Black women's sexuality, still largely invisible in literary texts. What might this mean for higher education curriculum content?

Black feminist key text readings continue to present new inclusive meanings in higher education following the groundbreaking works of several new scholars. Many are focused on using Black feminist theories in qualitative research, such as: Evans-Winters, 2019, Burkhard, 2022, and Porter et al., 2023. These Black feminist qualitative readings highlight the importance of Black feminist theory in the struggle to minimise racial and sexual discrimination in higher education. Such works have fostered anti-racist discussions centred on voice, other mothering, womanist learning, collaboration, activism, Black youth, and community.

Black British feminisms

The voices of Black British activist scholars, including those of Beverly Bryan, Stella Dadzie, and Susan Scafe in *The Heart of the Race* (1985), provide us with unique insights into the impact of Black British feminism and anti-racist action in the areas of community activism, community engagement, and social justice.

This volume celebrates Black British feminist perspectives in the work of: Suriya Nayak, Avtar Brah, Heidi Safia Mirza, Anne Phoenix,

Tracey Reynolds, and Gail Lewis, providing unique British insights into Black women's anti-racist, Black feminist experience in the United Kingdom. In particular, Black British feminist Heidi Safia Mirza who examined education's role in addressing race and gender inequalities. In *Race, Gender and Educational Desire* (Mirza, 2009), she explores Black women's educational experiences in Britain, while her 2019 co-edited volume, *Dismantling Race in Higher Education* (Arday and Miraz, 2018), focuses on decolonising academia and promoting equity. Both works highlight her commitment to transforming education for marginalised communities. in delivering Black feminist ideals in numerous areas of academia and community settings. To add to this, Gail Lewis (2017) stresses the need for anti-racist action in Black feminist activist work, allowing the nature of Black feminist sisterhood into the discourse (see Chapter 6, this volume).

The next chapter considers the usefulness of Black feminist text in intersecting oppressions of gender, sexuality, culture, and identity, and raises questions about curriculum content in higher education decolonising agendas. It also looks at sexuality, identity, and self, and the use of academic text for decolonising work in the higher education academy.

Learning objective

Assess how far decolonial feminism can assist us in bringing feminist voices together to tackle institutional change in decolonising higher education.

2

Using Black feminist text in the writing of the self

Acts of decolonisation in the writing of the self: sexuality and learner self-reflection in higher education

Joao Paulo Tinoco

Introducing reflection

> "se wo were fi na wosan kofa a yenki"
> [Peoples! Who said I walk alone? I am one only but never
> alone (Nunes, 2021).][1]

It is not a taboo to go back and reach for what you forgot (an Akan traditional proverb among peoples originating from Ghana, Togo, and Ivory Coast)

This chapter explores the writing of the self and engages with a decolonisation perspective. I focus my attention on storytelling and on the political uses of autobiographical writing, referred to as *autohistoria*, as a feminist exercise that is practised by women of colour, taking responsibility for the need to experience meeting points between the commitment to the articulation of an awareness of recognition and the urgencies of demands for social justice and collective.

I was awarded an overseas scholarship at Birkbeck, University of London, UK, and in 2022 I presented a research paper to the Womanism Activism Higher Education Research Network conference in March 2022.

Before starting my reflections, I believe it is important to salute the ancestral knowledge which I relate to. My creative power. They are voices that spoke before me. And at this moment I am writing, they emerge as if they were mine. As a candomblecist,[2] I understand the importance of valuing the knowledge that was left by our elders. I now embrace the *sankofa* process, as mentioned in the epigraph, to go back, back to my roots/past. The word *sankofa* means *sanko*, to go back, and *fa*, to reach, to bring. It is my ancestry: voices that precede me and give me the possibility of learning other viewpoints, other stories, (un)known experiences that emerge in this writing. I am one but never alone, the poet sings. Therefore, my wish is to be crossed and torn by the crossroad writing, to enter in-between places, so I can shake up practices that, because they are so familiar, go unnoticed.

This work is an attempt to explore key understandings of Black feminist ways while engaging largely with the groundbreaking work of Black feminist Gloria E. Anzaldúa. It explores the *use of dialogue as a means of assessing knowledge claims* and the value of using key text readings in decolonising work reflecting sexuality and "belonging". It is my belief that her work is vitally important in encouraging academia to experience decolonial perspectives in classrooms and other spaces of learning. I argue that Anzaldúa's notion of Borderlands – as a category that deconstructs the hegemony of the neoconservatives and breaks down labels and theories used to manipulate and control people – can offer other comprehensions of society and education, for example.

Anzaldúa (2015), in a letter addressed to women writers in the developing world. informs us of the paradox of writing. Anzaldúa, throughout her career and her writings, argues that writing is a way of telling versions of stories; it is narrative; it is different perceptions on the world; it is a way of rewriting stories about her, me, you, about us. Black women outside academia had to claim another perspective to promote their ideas and narratives, because they have their own powerful interpretations of their history. As Patricia Hill Collins (2000) points out, Black feminist theory is intertwined with a political and intellectual context which challenges its right to exist. What Collins explains pre-cisely is that the validation process of knowledge tends to be Eurocentric and that dominant groups hold the scientific author-ity, and they exclude other knowledge, for example, Black wom-en's knowledge.

However, every Black woman is a source of knowledge, once their living experience (wisdom) is considered a criterion of meaning (knowledge) (Collins, 2000). This notion is very close to the idea defended by Conceicao Evaristo of *escrevivência*, understood as a writing which is deeply committed to life and deeply committed to experience (Evaristo, 2017). It is also a way of empowering Black women to become sentinels, conveyers of witness, producers of histories. So, the pen becomes a weapon. It is a sword that renders the Black woman subject war prisoner in the intellectual mind factory (Anzaldúa, 2000).

Writing of this sense is the essence of meaningful relationships, that is, encounters, either with ourselves or with others. This process of encountering is what makes writing a bold gesture, because it is a courageous and political act: an act of resistance to exist. It is furthermore an act of decolonisation because it breaks the comfortable stereotypical images that White people have of "Third World" women.

Anzaldúa (2012) relates her own stories, and she exposes them before those who dare to read her life dissected by cuts that multiply, overflow, and intersect, and she refers to situations that are painful moments but with which the reader may identify and even feel complicit. Her stories sometimes focus on elements of everyday life; at other times they offer complex theoretical and epistemological proposals that challenge normative and colonial imaginaries.

In this sense, writing becomes a chain of discoveries, constructions, and achievements, exploring different perspectives of self-reflection, such as in Black feminist research practice.

Analysing Gloria Anzaldúa's understanding and approach to writing, I see it as a practice that reinvents and expands existing possibilities. Her perspective shows that as writers and researchers, we use words—written and/or spoken—not only to narrate realities but also to challenge and reshape them. In this sense, we can simultaneously embody both the academic, intellectual persona and the streetwise, lived experience. (Anzaldúa, 2000).

Aren't there times when we are full of anger or happiness, for instance, due to something we see or something that happens to us? Suddenly, we are urged into sharing those situations, combining these experiences as streetwise people at the same time as we can engage as a critic. However, you may read the same situation in a way that I, cis, male, White, gay, immigrant[3], candomblecist may not, because we inhabit different positions. Based on this, there will be people who will see themselves reflected in my writing and other people who will reflect on my ideas. This is the hope for a decolonising agenda in higher education academies: that readers will identify meaningful connections and patterns relevant to their experiences. In doing so, this production of knowledge fosters a bridge between the other and the self, inviting readers to integrate their own perspectives into the text.Therefore, this practice is based on the perspective of unlearning in order to learn as the way we learnt is already impregnated with a colonial logic. There are other ways of thinking about the world, and one of those options is the decolonial one.

To write about my own journey in this regard, a journey, pervaded by links, meetings, disagreements, questions, experiences, interests, problems, exchanges, theories, and political positions, I decided to divide my thoughts into two parts. In the first, I write about the theoretical-methodological-political choices assumed as the guiding choice of this writing. In the second, I discuss *autohistoria* as theorisation in Black feminist research practice.

Thus, the objective of this work is to reflect on the epistemic reconstruction perspective from the border. For this, I analyse Gloria Anzaldúa's work *Borderlands* (2012), which constructs a theory-practice *border*, attempting at best, to reject the hegemonic/colonial power through a heterogeneous ontology.

It is important to say that Anzaldúa (2012) did not find representation in White feminism. When considering the struggles of Black people, she noticed Black women's precise experiences tended to be under-represented, since by prioritising race, many specific issues involving gender and Black women's experiences, become invisible. In this sense, it is necessary to discuss the identities and the lived experiences of Black women, which cannot be reflected separately in the categories of racial discrimination or gender discrimination.

In this way, I resonate with Anzaldúa and other Black women feminist theorists, such as bell hooks, Conceição Evaristo, and Grada Kilomba. I am intertwined in this process of analysis-writing as if it were a testimony in which the victim becomes a witness, and the latter becomes the victim. Testimony involves the act of sharing experiences and the possibility of seeing oneself reflected in them. It includes speaking as a victim to (d)enounce vicissitudes from the position of a subject articulating their discourse.

I now turn to a discussion of Anzaldúa's work, and some of her reflections.

Gloria E. Anzaldúa: The writing as a theoretical crossing

Gloria E. Anzaldúa was a feminist author, activist, lesbian, and professor. Indigenous and Chicana, woman of colour, Anzaldúa experiences the in-between-place-*fronterizo* between Mexico and the United States of America. Her writing scratches the page like a razor, leaving the paper red and Black. Her hands, like goose feathers, are "peopled" with absences that seek, in writing, a relationship with the other and with herself, giving space to a pulse, a desire to overflow fragments of identifications in which the Chicana/Indigenous woman is inscribed, naming her the *mestiza*.

The *mestiza* is the construction of the Chicana/Indigenous woman subject who no longer feels comfortable in silence. She speaks her mind: about her feelings, dreams and plans, her sexual desires, struggles and conquests, her desire for power without hierarchies. The *mestiza* is a feminist and values her past and present, forgives her faults, and has the courage to continue. She bleeds. She bleeds to find her colonial trauma and, in this way, deconstructs it so that the *herida*[4] can be healed. If it is possible to be healed. Everything is so uncertain. The healing leaves scars. The *mestiza* is in a warlike place, where the colonial power creates strategies to silence the border people, people on the margin (Anzaldúa, 2012).

First, we need to understand what coloniality is. Coloniality is a concept that reveals the logical trace of Western civilisation, its formation, and the global expansion since the sixteenth century.

There is a distinction between coloniality and decolonisation (or, if you prefer, decoloniality). Coloniality, as I have already said, is linked to the common logic within Western colonial thought that I also acknowledge as hegemonic power.

Decolonisation, on the other hand, is the border between coloniality and decolonisation; however, its sociohistorical slant is analytical and critical in relation to colonisation. Analytical decolonisation is at once the history of the production of practices, transformation, control, and resistance. The analytical slant is one part of decolonisation, the other is praxis, the action that guides and directs towards (r)existence (Mignolo and Walsh, 2018).

This construction of acting, thinking in action – there is no reflection without apprehending practice – that I write here underlines Anzaldúa's memories left on the page through ancestors' voices, specifically the work *Borderlands/La frontera: The New Mestiza* (Anzaldúa, 2012), producing in me a spiritual desire that comes from my incompleteness regarding the dichotomous practices that are inscribed and materialised in the voices that preceded me. I mean spiritual in the sense of desiring changes, completeness, and (trans)formations of knowledge that are produced in and by the centre. I emphasise that even if completeness is an illusory condition, it is also necessary to produce knowledge. The production is research, which is the encounter with the scientific areas, with the subjects, it is a set of choices that together define the methodological path taken to achieve the objective of (in)forming, knowing.

According to Walter Mignolo (2008), the decolonial option means thinking from the outside and in a subaltern epistemic position vis-à-vis the epistemic hegemony that creates, builds, and erects an outside to ensure its interiority.

This subaltern *episteme* that goes beyond the border is interested in demarcating the position from where the critic builds their thoughts and the colonial differences which are linked to their biographical sensibilities (Mignolo, 2012).

These biographical sensibilities build the border between the epistemological and geohistorical knowledge. It is necessary, according to Edgar Nolasco (2013), that the critic of the border landscape should be predisposed to think from the border marks, from the local and biographical sensibilities of the subjects and the productions of the place, from the memories, discourses and knowledge, languages, from local histories that were silenced by the colonisation of power (Nolasco, 2013).

I argue that Anzaldúa does not write only for women, although her main objective is to communicate/bridge with them, especially with Chicana/Indigenous/Black women: *las mestizas*, or those of mixed-race identity. Anzaldúa's conception of bridge, for instance, invites us to understand Black women's writings as a mediator between themselves and their community, and White people, feminists, and lesbians. They select which group to bridge with, or we choose them. That may happen consciously or unconsciously. In Anzaldúa's writings there is an invitation to subjects who are at the border. For example, I am gay and experience exclusion through heteronormative practices, and/or sometimes the coloniality mindset questions my religion, which is an African diasporic one, saying it is "devil worship". It is important to say that my position is not to make any kind of representation of the author. I write *from* Anzaldúa, *from* her *writings*.

This practice of writing also leads me to (my) absences. I write by incorporating myself, and (de)constructing new ways of thinking based on Anzaldúa's narratives. It is a theorisation that is built by writing which seeks the necessary theoretical threads that dialogue with the production of this chapter.

That said, it is important that I explain some notions that will guide this work. These are notions such as discourse and subject for Discourse Analysis (DA), the geohistorical site (Nolasco, 2013), *autohistoria* (Anzaldúa, 2015), and the *Border Episteme* (Anzaldúa, 2012). It is worth mentioning that this work is crossed with the decolonial aim (Anzaldúa, 2012; Colchado, 2020).

To think about the decolonial conditions in which they are represented by the critical productions of Southern studies (Mignolo, 2012; Nolasco, 2013; Santos, 2010), I believe it is important to explain how I understand the discourse and the subject. From the perspective of transdisciplinary DA, I find in Michel Foucault (2014) the study of discourse to apprehend the construction of the subject and the complexity of discontinuous factors in history that are constitutive of them.

In *Archaeology of Knowledge* (2014), Foucault exposes an archival study of the excavation of discourses, formulating concepts and methodological procedures that help me, as a discourse analyst, to understand the production of subjectivity and the subject. These productions are generated in the relationship between language and history because the latter determines the possibilities of realising the former.

The discourse is the relationship between A and B. It is the possibility of producing significant effects that emerge in the conflicting space of what is similar and different at the same time. Discourse is external to language, but it is dependent on language for its material existence, sometimes in texts, sometimes in images, under historical-social determinations. The subject and the Geohistorical Site reveal in which social situation the subject is crossed; their lexical and image choices are tracked by the discourse analyst, leading us to understand more about a subject.

The Geohistorical Site is a term used by Edgar Cézar Nolasco (2013) to refer to a place that roots local stories and that helps me to exhume veiled memories; archives that collect memories that are waiting to be exposed. These files are the sets of discourses (utterances) in which the subject is submerged. In it, the utterances are encapsulated, waiting anxiously to be (re) used. The subject acts and thinks through discourse, which dictates and authorises the necessary and possible utterances (Foucault, 2014).

For example, the work *Borderlands* (2012) can be seen as a regular set of linguistic facts that are crossed by polemics and strategies, that is, there is a power relationship that permeates the subject-writer, the subject being an effect of subjectivity. The subject has the illusion that the words are theirs and they seek only one truth. It is known that language is not transparent once the ideological veil is so familiar that we cannot notice it.

The discourse, therefore, is what establishes what must be said and what moment it must be said, since the Geohistorical Site

(Nolasco, 2013) of the subject legitimises the voices that emerge from that specific place. This reveals the heterogeneity of the subject. In other words, the subject enunciates voices that precede them, distant, pre-constructed voices, captured throughout their lives and experience. These voices are updated, opening to the construction of other senses of meaning.

I would like to demonstrate this sense of meaning with the word *Chicano*, for instance. This same term is likely to reveal other interpretations, hidden by the choice of one term among others, which annuls other ones. The word *Chicano* at the beginning of its use referred to the Mexican-North American/Indigenous peoples as uncultured, lower-class peoples. In *Borderlands* (2012), Anzaldúa presents the same term with a different meaning, that is, a political position that claims justice and equality for the Chicano/Indigenous peoples.

In addition, the term *Chicana* achieves other senses of meaning from what Anzaldúa (2012) proposes, referring to the Mexican-North American/Indigenous woman on the border, in-between borders, in-between places, between languages and, cultures. Therefore, the senses of meaning emerge when considering the specific place from where the subject speaks – and that the subject speaks at a given moment and not another. It is with the importance and urgency of this in mind that I ask the following question: How did the writing of *Borderlands* (2012) appear at a certain moment and no other book appear in its place?

There was an urgency in raising the voices of women of colour. A decolonising agenda had emerged, and, tired of always hearing people writing and speaking of her, Anzaldúa (2012) wrote an essay to tell her stories and the history of her Chicano people, building a theory of the border. It was a theory that was thought outside the big centres to reject the reflections that excluded peoples are marginalised. Giving students opportunities to self-reflect through Black feminist studies, for instance, is a tool to encourage the other to listen to truths we as White people want to turn away from or keep at a distance, at the margins, unnoticed, and silenced. The way Anzaldúa chooses to face and show these masks is through her writing.

This research practice choice is produced to reveal not only the paths taken during the investigation process, but it also configures itself as a political act, since, when doing research, we are making it explicit which assumptions guide our practices. Therefore, our choices are based on a perspective that considers that knowledge is socially and historically located and that it is constructed together with other subjects who are directly and indirectly involved in the research (Anzaldúa, 2012; 2015).

Anzaldúa (2012) directs her gaze through an intersectional feminist perspective. That is, she seeks to analyse and understand the differentiated power relations that place Black women in unequal positions. Intersectionality, a category that emerged in Global South Black feminism, is used by her with the aim of relating different systems of power and oppression that operate in the lives of women, especially Black women, without hierarchising which one is more important.

Anzaldúa's writing (2012) at some point cuts the reader off, and in her writing, she provides the threads for the suture. Her revolt in the writing of Borderlands (2012) appears as a cathartic effect, an instrument of healing her psychic wounds, not only Anzaldúa's wounds but also the *heridas* of those who have her writings in their hands.

How her writings reach the other is possible due to similar occurrences that the subjects find themselves through the stories. It is as if the reader were unveiling individual and collective memories, becoming a reader-author once they recognise their own experiences and/or narratives. Memory emerges as a palimpsest, always returning to the palimpsest – memories of previous memories – ready to be (re)emerged in other moments and historical contexts.

These other discursive memories are what Anzaldúa (2015) calls *autohistoria*: the history of history, the history of the subject, and the history of culture; self to the I-enunciator. *Autohistoria* is connection. For instance, we can think of *autohistoria* when Christina Sharpe (2016) metaphors the foam left by the ship in the wake in the Atlantic Ocean as stories that need to be told; or when Conceição Evaristo (2019) writes a poem that narrates the passage of a ship through the Kalunga[5] sea, which witnessed the death of the dead not so dead; or when the hands of bell hooks (1995) formulate the method in which Black women can meld with crafting practice to (de)construct other perspectives.

Torres (2005) explains that Anzaldúa's *autohistoria* has already become a canonical text when it comes to North American border studies; it was, and most likely continues to be, the most cited theoretical work in studies on the incessant coming and going of bicultural subjects from Hispanic communities in the United States, those who live on the borders, the deterritorialised ones.

In the preface to *Borderlands*, first published in 1987, Anzaldúa motivates other authors to apply her theory from any enunciative site, for example, the Geohistorical Site (Nolasco, 2013), since visible and invisible borders are established globally.

In Anzaldúa's *autohistoria* (2012), the writing of the self, there is a rooted desire for change as a mission to be accomplished. The *autohistoria* emerges from the breadth of scope through various stories told by Chicana/Indigenous women, women of colour, who live or have lived through the same conflicts as Anzaldúa. The *autohistoria* has the desire to hear the screams that are silenced. It is the invitation to gather the pieces of writing which unveil the tormentors' teeth and create other ways of building femininities, demanding the right to exist, building bridges of empathy in counterpoint to the premeditated individualism and arrogance forged in the harvest of Whiteness (Alves, 2021).

It is the oral and the written, the story and the tale, the fact and the fiction, the theory and practice, in the autobiographical and historiographical narrative, in addition to recounting in the writing personal and family experiences that together form and illustrate the complex collective experience of the female condition.

To this end, this line of argument suggests that it is essential to deconstruct the very concept of objectivity as it is traditionally understood within the framework of modern knowledge systems. From this perspective, deconstructing objectivity challenges its presumed neutrality, a quality often attributed to it by the constructivist sciences, and instead reveals it as inherently shaped by partial perspectives and biases.

Thus, in feminist research, for example, subjectivity is achieved when one recognises the places where they find themselves and where they started from – which is one's own body and not a neutral "nowhere".

Based on Chicana/Indigenous literature-theory, Anzaldúa sees *autohistoria* as a term that she herself uses to describe a genre of writing a story of someone that is both personal and collective, using fictional elements, something between a memoir and fictionalised autobiography (Keating, 2005).

This way of writing signalises the text of *Borderlands* (2012) by Gloria Anzalùda. The text is written as a biographical discourse in which she considers her biography and the biography of her people, creating a cultural and political space where Chicana/Indigenous women can have their position and representation rather than separating realities.

Lea Colchado (2020), a Texan and a Chicana, interprets autohistoria as a process of creating spaces for Chicana traumatic narratives. Characterized by elements like magical thinking, it engages with shadows, myths, theory, and spiritual activism, setting it apart from traditional autobiographical models. Autohistoria's distinctiveness also lies in its naming, which uses a language other than standard English. This approach allows mestiza women to incorporate bilingual and bicultural theoretical foundations, offering unique possibilities for exploring traumatic mestiza narratives that other autobiographical genres cannot provide. I defend with Colchado (2020) and Anzaldúa (2012) that notion that *autohistoria* is the contention that women can navigate their own traumas. According to Colchado (2020), Anzaldúa did not leave a ready-made methodology for *autohistoria*, as she believed that *autohistorias* were always in a process of creation and change, constantly changing and growing from different perceptions of knowledge.

AnaLouise Keating (2005) organised some characteristics that make up *autohistoria*, whether it is related to individuality and togetherness, self-reflection, culture, or politics, as well as the incorporation of local knowledge and displacement of dualities in the narrative. *Autohistoria* focuses on everyday life stories and theoretical dimensions.

From this *autohistoria* perspective, especially in *Borderlands* (Anzalùda, 2012), I see a (dis)connection that the author generates with the story of her life. The fictional movement overlaps with the experience, in the process of which the experience becomes fiction.

The writing of the self, elaborated by Foucault (2014), corresponds not only to the registration of the self but also constitutes the subject itself, performing the notion of the subject. Self-knowledge is not synonymous with history itself; rather, history surrounds us, shaping and constraining our experiences. However, history does not define who we are—it reveals how we differ from its constraints and from dominant narratives. This difference emerges as we reinterpret history to challenge fixed identities and embrace the multiplicity of who we are becoming. History, therefore, dissipates rigid notions of identity, allowing space for transformation into the "other" we continually become. Anzaldúa refers to this process of representation and re-identification—where new narratives and meanings emerge—as *autohistoria*, a form of self-writing that engages with these complexities. This type of action at universities, for example, is important to dislodge and deconstruct certain policies and practices. In the country in which I was born, a law was introduced which required the teaching of Afro-Brazilian and African history and culture. Educating "our people with our history" was important to combat racism and recognised the contribution that Black people have made in building our society, a topic that is treated in the classroom with superficiality and stereotypes. The law had been in place for 20 years in 2023, and we still struggle to put the law into practice across Brazil. Worldwide, the decolonising agenda was gathering strength.

The writing of the self, under *autohistoria*, possesses a transformative power of reflection and change that deeply impacts us. This impact occurs in different ways—sometimes for those writing, as they inscribe their experiences and identities into the text, and sometimes for those reading, as they are challenged and provoked by the meanings that (e)merge from the writing. This process of crossing us refers to how *autohistoria* traverses personal and collective boundaries, creating profound connections and insights. It is a space of discoveries of the self-discovery and self-reflection about life and experiences, since these actions can transform the subject into a better observer/researcher. *Autohistoria* emerges from this place where there are impediments to connecting with ourselves, unable to communicate with realities and true values for us. The writing of *autohistoria* is a way of identifying with different subjects (Anzaldúa, 2012).

Nolasco (2004) quoting Roland Barthes (1975), states that the writer is inscribed in fiction as a character drawn in the writing itself, building a fable that competes with the work. It is a miscegenation in which the making of life, a fable, is more than reading Anzaldúa's life as a text, her biography, life, and writing: it is to perceive the value of life and work and read all of that at the same time.

The writing of the self, according to our author, manages to cross the limit of what we are in the space of in-between places, that is, the intersubjective place of exchange of *autohistoria* and community. In this way, the *autohistoria* genre can be understood as an ongoing process—a form of writing that embraces incompleteness and reflects a constant desire to detach from fixed identities. It offers no rest from the (de)construction of self, encouraging continual reflection, transformation, and reinterpretation of personal and collective narratives.

Autohistoria is a way of experiencing self-esteem, refusing to being tokenised. Anzaldúa draws our attention to understanding the relationship of pleasure and self-esteem with the Black body, when Black women's memories are built through negative aspects that went through colonisation, enslavement, and post-abolition. In her childhood, one of her memories, Anzaldúa (2012) says, is that she always heard that her language was wrong. Through various attacks, her native language was belittled, devaluing it as belonging to an Indigenous woman of colour. She was told this by arrogant racist teachers who considered all Chicano children dumb and dirty. That was another reason to become a teacher of English. In the words of our writer, "I will no longer be made to feel ashamed of existing. I will have my voice: Indian, Spanish, White. I will have my serpent's tongue – my woman's voice, my sexual voice, my poet's voice. I will overcome the tradition of silence" (Anzaldúa, 2012, p. 81).

Norma Alarcón (1990) points out that the central axes that mark the emergence of Chicana writing are characterised by a strong insistence on implementing exercises linked to self-determination, from which processes of self-invention emerge in the interstices of various cultures. The cultural, symbolic, and subjective processes interlaced together, exposed by the *mestiza*, configure a set of imaginary axes from which it is possible to articulate such identification processes that sustain the dichotomous contours on which the boundaries between Anglo and Mexican are founded, dismantling the racialised and colonial bases that support the imaginaries that make up the social hierarchies on the border.

According to Anzaldúa (2015), there is a need to deepen this reflection, instead of continuing to reproduce the models that we have been offered by the research efforts of the social sciences. That is the reason we need to establish listening and reporting spaces for Black women. Grada Kilomba writes in her book *Plantation Memories* (2020) that Black women have rarely been the subjects. In her words:

> This position of objecthood that we commonly occupy, this place of "Otherness", does not, as commonly believed, indicate a lack of resistance or interest, but rather a lack of access to representation on the part of Blacks themselves. It is not that we have not been speaking, but rather our voices – through a system of racism – have been either systematically disqualified as

invalid knowledge; or else represented by *whites* who, ironically, become the "experts" on ourselves. (p. 26)

Thus, Black women are faced with a set of discursive practices that, through the rescue and articulation of different discourses and stories, dispute places from which it is possible for this hegemonic voice to emerge, circulate, and create ways of naming, challenging people at the border to break the silence imposed by hegemonic literature.

Anzaldúa's appeal in developing the notion of *autohistoria* is to argue that Chicana/Indigenous/Black women have a voice. It is important that they learn the significance of knowing how to express themselves, allowing them to be invaded by a desire for transformations through the writing and, it is to be hoped, giving them the courage to relate their experiences of trauma, oppression, and resistance in their everyday lives. This way of expressing oneself, or even the writing of the self, allows one to question their feelings as a production of self that can be (re) thought in various ways. *Autohistoria* allows the subject not only to demonstrate her knowledge but also to put that knowledge into practice.

Here we ought to reflect on Anzaldúa's contributions related to Black feminism and decolonial studies (2012), highlighting a responsibility to share points of view by and for Black women. Black feminism, as a political and social justice movement, discusses specificities that affect the lives of Black women in order to make their experience a better world, addressing systemic issues such as racism, sexism, and economic inequality while advocating for intersectional approaches to social change. According to Patricia Hill Collins (2019), from this perspective, the contributions of Black intellectuals are essential to foster new models aimed at promoting social change.

The writing of these Black women – literary and/or theoretical – when creating possibilities to rethink, recreate, and intervene in the social dynamics, positions them as intellectuals, because they represent, embody, and articulate a message, point of view, act, philosophy, or opinion.

The writing of Black women, constructed from their perspective and experience, is analysed as a form of activism. We must change the idea that activism is "concrete" actions, for example, acts in the street. The intellectuality linked to the mental work, which is so important and useful for the revolutionary struggle, has its position devalued, since these efforts are not "visible" immediately (hooks, 1995).

Autohistoria, therefore, deconstructs stereotyped images and reformulates Black women's own identities. In this case, *autohistoria* discusses the intellectuality of Black women as a proposal for epistemological change and rescue, no longer as bodies objectified and represented by, but rather as subjects of their own creations and stories.

Autohistoria as theorisation: A concept for the practice of telling stories

To demonstrate this process of *autohistoria*, I cite an excerpt from Anzaldúa in her book *Borderlands* (Anzaldùa, 2012) to show her reflection towards her cultural and linguistic *locus*, resisting the colonial criticism that insists on imprinting on border bodies its modes of subjectivation. Anzaldúa (2012) outlines the trajectories of Mexicans, (in)famous subjects, marked by a bad reputation through categories of abnormality, as well as by the oblivion of their biographies through history. She fulminates against the tradition which sees Mexicans as:

> Faceless, nameless, invisible, taunted with "Hey *cucaracho*" (cockroach). Trembling with fear yet filled with courage, a courage born of desperation. Barefoot and uneducated, Mexicans with hands like boot soles gather at night by the river where two worlds merge creating what Reagan calls a frontline, a war zone. (Anzaldúa, 2012, p. 33)

The Chicano/Indigenous people have a tradition of migration, a tradition of long walks. Currently, the Chicano/Indigenous people witness *la migración de los pueblos mexicanos,*)returning from the odyssey to *Aztlán*, the historical and mythological site. This time, the path is from south to north. This return to the promised land began with the Indigenous people in the interior of Mexico and with the *mestizos* who came with the colonisers in the 1500s. The convergence created a culture shock, a cultural border, and a closed country (Anzaldúa, 2012).

Immigration continued for the next three centuries with the *braceros*, the peasants, who helped build the train tracks and harvest fruits and vegetables. Today, thousands of Mexicans are crossing the border between Mexico and the United States, both legally and illegally. Ten million undocumented people have returned to the south, to Mexico, Guatemala, Brazil, and Bolivia, among other Latin American countries (Anzaldúa, 2012).

The discourse is always linked to the historical conditions of production, to the discursive memory crossed by other voices, and to subjectivity, emerging senses of meaning that erupt through the discursive thread (Almeida, 2019; Guerra, 2017). Therefore, women of colour unveil a chase scenario, where obstacles are placed ready to catch the prey. The hegemonic power is the bait. This group in power is blessed. On this side we have those who want to be blessed too but are not welcome, because on this side of the border we are faceless, nameless, invisible, barefoot, and uneducated people.

I analyse the occurrences of adjectives in the utterance speech, which characterise an imaginary knowledge of the Chicana/Indigenous subject. A practice of exclusion emerges, in which the marks of the margin form the border, maintained by erasing the collective memory of the excluded.

The use of adjectives, such as invisible, insulted, *cucaracho*, barefoot, and uncultured, aims to address the conditions in which human life becomes possible and the conditions in which human life becomes difficult, even impossible. There is an idyllic imaginary of equality in society regarding the possibility of life. However, among Chicano, Indigenous, and Black people, the conditions also refer to superiority and inferiority, to inequality in life (Moreno, 2005).

Segregation is articulated by the illusion of symmetry. Symmetry shows how the subject is different in its difference, how any difference that is signified in society and history is not symmetrical.

In other words, the false expectation of symmetry makes every difference appear a deformation or mutilation. In this logic, the subject cannot signify in the place of the other, and through their difference, without symmetry, which asserts their subject-position, socially and politically constituted, that is, it is through dissymmetry that the Chicana/Indigenous woman resists.

With a bit of irony, not to say a lot, and anger, Anzaldúa (2012) reports that US police officers, who patrol the border between Mexico and the United States, would hide behind McDonald's restaurants in Texas, or any other franchise in a border town to look for *crossers*. They set traps on the banks of the river, specifically under bridges. Hunters dressed in green uniforms looked for economic refugees using an electronic sensor that could see them at night.

Cornered by the lanterns, panicking as their hands were over their heads, *los mojados*, illegal immigrants wet from crossing the river, were handcuffed, strapped into jeeps, and returned to the other side of the border. They are the invisible, insulted, *cucarachos*, the barefoot and uneducated ones, thrown beyond fences made of barbed wire, trembling with fear, at night by the river where two worlds connect (Anzaldúa, 2012).

That is the reason literary narratives produced by Black women help us to understand the atrocities of racism, a violent reality, that for centuries has silenced voices that attempt to contest it. It is a strong argument in favour of the necessity of a change of perspective for the subject who lives the reality to speak with their own voice (Kilomba, 2020). Women of colour have found in literary writing a way to autohistoricise themselves and to rewrite the history of a nation project, where once they were narrated from the perspective of the White man,[6] heterosexual and belonging to an elite economic.

It is in the look of the other that one is challenged, and that the Chicana/Indigenous woman perceives the signs of identification and estrangement. Identification and estrangement occur due to the illusion that the subject has of being the owner of themselves, of their will and choices. When the other says: "you have no name" or "you have no face", the desire to have a name and a face is generated. The estrangement is observed by the lack of completeness. In turn, the identification is through the difference: "They have a face and I do not".

The Chicana/Indigenous critique is noticed from the outside, from the in-between space which is formulated on the border. This aim, under the *autohistoria* notion, proposes a deconstruction of a dualist reading, in which senses of meaning guide what is said by the centre, that must be accepted without questioning the voice of the Chicane/Indigenous woman which is part of a rebellious movement that transcends a new epistemological terrain, that is, *autohistoria*.

The wounds that (still) bleed

In this chapter, I explore Black feminist perspectives through the writings of Gloria Anzaldúa, focusing on the experiences of Chicana/Indigenous women and women of color. Anzaldúa's work, particularly in *Borderlands* (2012), examines the act of self-writing as a means of documenting history and personal experiences. Her text delves into the concept of living on the border, embracing a process of rebellious self-identification while confronting and narrating personal traumas.

This rebellious movement is provoked by the desire for completeness, lucubration, (dis)satisfaction, and dreams that confess the mutability of identity, leaving their traces scattered – and followed by me as a discourse analyst through the heterogeneous constituency of the Chicana/Indigenous woman subject, for example.

I believe that these reflections on these issues are relevant because, in the field of linguistics, there are only a few works that problematise, describe, interpret, and analyse Anzaldúa's literary discourse, as well as discursive representations that revolve around silenced identities, social inequality, and exclusion via DA.

Thus, I wanted to bring to these pages the gesture of interpretation that I make of the work *Borderlands* (Anzalùda, 2012), as a decolonising choice, to discuss strategies to overcome gender, race, and class inequalities and the various forms of coloniality. It is an invitation to unleash our passion for social justice because there is a wave which keeps putting barriers around knowledge and history.

The senses of meaning are landscapes. It is up to us to observe and photograph these movements. It is noted that the Chicana/Indigenous woman confronts discourses from the official history, legitimised discourses and (re)produced by the common sense through the population towards marginalised culture, in which they are stereotyped as *primitive/delayed*.

At the border, the gender intersection, class, and race/ethnicity continue to define social subaltern places. After going through resignifications and (re)editions, racism and patriarchy still act with strong traces of the past. Economic and social differences remain glaring. These differences, reproduced for generations and generations, occur also through the persistence of racial and gender discrimination.

Therefore, problematising this theme is necessary, since today's society discusses a social change regarding minorities, and excluded groups, and, often, we do not know the history from the point of view of the *fronterizos* subjects, such as Black women, the landless, illiterate people, gays, lesbians, transvestites, transsexuals, bisexuals, riverside dwellers, immigrants, convicts, and so on.

The challenge remains for everyone, especially for us who are trying to break the chains through our research practice, to understand this intersection and its consequences, seeking to combat inequality and discrimination, tracing an effective way to contribute to the construction of an equitable society following the directions given by Black women.

And if we allow ourselves to be touched by this ancestral knowledge, always collective, always attentive to injustice, we will be closer to building powerful bridges towards decolonisation. It is not about idealising the past but realising the past in us, even though the colonial power keeps telling us the opposite. This chapter is intertwined in a continuous circle where everything is in the process of (trans)formation. It is the past, present, and future. It is ancestry. Black feminist research practice is a tension that links experiences and ideas, which results in the connection between experiences (as a heterogeneous activity) and collective knowledge arising from an associated point of view. There is a space between the individual, heterogeneous and the collective experience (marked by common experiences). There is also a connection between Black feminist practice and Black feminist notions which contrasts with the dialectical relationship that connects oppression to activism and with the dialogical relationship between collective experiences and the production of group knowledge. In other words, it is the challenge of creating connections between the experiences of Black women as a collective heterogeneous group and views of other oppressed groups. These are the factors that make writing, for instance, a strategy for subverting the system; a wish to heal the wounds; a way of creating a fertile ground for the coming generations of women and men of colour and White students.

I highlighted the importance of the Black, mestizo, Indian, peripheral, and lesbian (non-binary) narrative in the writing of the self not only as a description of the vicissitudes of those who resist the oppressive and paralysing heterosexual structures of the patriarchal system that camouflage, defend, and strengthen asymmetrical power relations, but to contribute to the review of hegemonic discourses. It is in the writing of the self that Black women's survival lies, because according to Anzaldúa, a woman who writes has power, and a woman with power is feared. Writing and reading contribute to this achievement, and to the articulation of these dimensions, through an *autohistoria* perspective, situating and disseminating counter-hegemonic knowledges at schools and in universities.

The trace of the ink on the paper is the path which will lead us to bridges which connect us emotionally, socially, politically, and academically. As a White person, a male, I continue to resist the modern-day rules of colonial domination. Teaching and learning decolonial strategies are transformative, and learner self-reflection in Black feminist research allows us to change the detrimental narratives embedded in Eurocentric literature and other educational platforms. In an attempt to educate myself, I am trying to do my homework and keep up the urge to go back to my ancestors and project it towards my writing, my research, our research, so we can move forward to build a strong, Black feminist rhetoric and attend to our responsibilities in the struggle. I must now collect the pieces.

The following chapter examines the contested spaces of personal identity through the perspective of a White middle-class tutor who becomes a mixed-race ally. Drawing inspiration from Black feminist epistemology, this tutor engages with liberating and decolonising education programmes, particularly those aimed at improving access to British higher education for underrepresented and marginalised groups..

Learning objective

Understand the value of Black feminist text in the higher education decolonising curriculum.

Theme Two: Sharing good practice in using Black feminist theory in higher education decolonising work

3
Decolonising from the margins

Centring tutor identity and Black feminist thought in higher education

Sue Dunn

Introduction

In this chapter, I use an ethnography approach to chart my journey from a White-identifying research biochemist to a mixed-race lecturer in social science. In using a narrative approach, I explore how experiences of classist and sexist behaviours led me to become an educationalist and gave rise to an understanding of intersectionality. I consider how progressive educational policies can be sabotaged by hegemonic barriers and how change is most effectively instigated from the margins of the institution. The chapter concludes by proposing a decolonising pedagogy that draws on Black feminist theory that values students' and tutors' multiple identities and brings these into teaching and learning.

bell hooks (1994), writing of her teachers in her all-Black school, says: "Although they did not define or articulate these practices in theoretical terms, my teachers were enacting a revolutionary pedagogy that was profoundly anticolonial" (p. 2). This passage resonates with me. As I look back over my early career as a teacher, it describes my approach, unarticulated as it was. I have never regarded myself as enacting a revolutionary pedagogy, but I now realise that I have spent much of my personal and professional life working for social change and challenging hegemonic assumptions, often from the edges of the academy.

Drawing on the work of Hunt (2009), I take an autoethnographic approach and look at how my identity grew and expanded from a White, middle-class child brought up in rural England to a mixed heritage decolonial feminist teaching in the UK capital city. In exploring my influences and educational experiences through a life story approach, I show how growing up in a middle-class, White society enabled me to apply my understanding of class to gender, race, and colonialism in my professional life as a teacher. Three themes emerged from this act of critical analysis. Firstly, I saw how repeatedly, progressive educational policies that tried to enhance equality and social justice floundered on hegemonic beliefs of those empowered to implement them.

Secondly, I uncovered how change must by necessity arise from the margins of the academy. Any organisation that functions successfully within its own terms, has little incentive for change and innovation. For as long as entry to higher education was limited to around 10–12 per cent of 18-year-olds (Bolton, 2012), there was no drive to change admissions practise. Universities had the pick of applicants with appropriate grades and available places were filled. It is only through working in the margins of the tertiary education sector with marginalised students that I and others like me have been able to initiate change.

Finally, in analysing my practice as a teacher, I show how my decolonial feminist principles emerged in Black feminist perspectives. I recognised that key features in Patricia Hill Collins's Black feminist thought (Collins, 2000) can be drawn upon to counter the power imbalances and hegemonic assumptions in pedagogic practice. I learnt how, in sharing aspects of my identity, I was able to support students' learning in both biological sciences and social science. Developing this further, I end this chapter by proposing a Black feminist, decolonising pedagogy that recognises students as individuals, as agents in their own lives, engaging with each in a dialogue where learning can take place.

Beginnings – A privileged child unaware of race

I was brought up largely by my mother and maternal grandmother with some input from my mother's sister, in a small village where my family had lived for several generations. My father was an RAF officer and only came home intermittently on leave. I wasn't aware that my father was a different colour from everyone else I knew for many years. It was never referred to by anyone, so I didn't see skin colour; he was just my dad. I remember asking him once, when I was five or six years old, why he was a brown colour, and he told me he had fallen into a fire when he was small. I was too young to do anything other than accept it, though I did wonder whether it had hurt a lot and why didn't he have any scars. Everyone in the village, in my local school, and in the rest of my family was White, and so I regarded myself as such and was never made to feel different or Other. I only gradually became aware that one-half of my family lived in India when I was encouraged to write to my cousins and godparents.

My father came from the Anglo-Indian community and travelled to England to study aeronautical engineering when he was 19 years old. Anglo-Indians, formerly called Eurasians (Macaes, 2018), form a distinct community within India and have been much written about (Griffiths, 2013; Hedin, 1934; Zapate, 2018). Anglo-Indians trace their paternal ancestry back to European traders and colonisers in India, probably from the seventeenth century onwards (Dalrymple, 2003; Hedin, 1934). Being neither Indian nor European, Anglo-Indians became a distinct community and maintain a Europe-facing Christian culture. With English as their mother tongue and European names, they were privileged under the British Raj, despising ordinary Indians, and imbued with a sense of cultural superiority. They exemplified the principle laid down by Macaulay in 1883: "We must do our best to form a class who may be interpreters between us and the millions whom we govern: a class of persons, Indians in blood and colour, but English in taste, in opinions and in intellect" (Macaulay, 1835, p.9). Although this principle was intended to create a class of Indians to administer the British empire (Tharoor, 2018, p. 186), it was fully inculcated into the Anglo-Indian community. Thus, my father, in common with other Anglo-Indians of his generation, regarded themselves as British, culturally and socially.

It was only several decades later that I realised the depth of racism my father must have experienced as a brown-skinned man arriving in England in the 1930s, when an aunt told me, many years after Dad passed away, that he was "always so dignified when he walked out of a restaurant that had refused to serve him". He came from a very privileged background as an Anglo-Indian, and as a senior RAF officer, he expected and received considerable respect from everyone who knew him. He never discussed race with me, and I was unaware of anything that could be called racism directed towards him or myself. My mother must have been very brave to have married him, probably against her family's wishes.

Class distinctions

Although issues of race passed me by entirely as a child, class and class distinctions were and continue to be all-pervasive in rural England.

Class distinctions were certainly enacted at my primary school, a small rural school with about 50 pupils. In the final year of primary school, I encountered the Eleven- Plus (11-plus) examination. The outcome of the 11-plus exam determined whether a child went to the secondary modern school or to a single-sex grammar school. At my small primary school, however, access to the 11-plus exam, and hence the opportunity to progress to a grammar school, was not universally available. There were around seven of us in my age cohort, three with parents with professional backgrounds, and the rest from mainly agricultural labouring families. But only we three middle-class kids were prepared for the 11-plus, taught separately, and given practice papers to work on for several months ahead of the test. The deeply engrained class beliefs of my teachers, all White middle-class women, gave them the right to deny the opportunity for an academic education to those children considered unsuitable.

This appeared to have been a common practice according to Gristy, Letherby and Watkins (2019):

> In some areas, children sat qualifying tests in their school to determine who went forward to sit the final examination, with head teachers wielding significant, if not total control, over who took the 11+, often basing this decision upon a perception of who was likely to pass (Watkings 2019, p. 164).

This must be the earliest example I encountered of hegemonic social and cultural beliefs acting to sabotage progressive educational initiatives. I would encounter similar ingrained attitudes on gender and class as I grew older.

Celebrating comprehensive school education

I was spared the all-girls grammar school as the comprehensive system was introduced in Hampshire just as I was moving from primary to secondary schooling. The purpose of the introduction of comprehensive education was to "reorganise secondary education on comprehensive lines which will preserve all that is valuable in grammar school education for those children who now receive it and make it available to more children" (Department of Education and Science, 1965).

The local secondary modern school was decanted into smart new buildings and rebranded as a Comprehensive School with a grammar school entry into the first year.

Despite the progressive objectives of comprehensive education, the class segregation persisted. Although the physical space created by the new comprehensive school was occupied by pupils from a range of socio-economic classes, the educational spaces were as rigidly fixed as when the secondary modern and grammar schools were several miles apart. Streaming of pupils seemed to be based on class, as the two pupils from my primary school who had sat the 11-plus but failed were both in the same "A" stream with me. My other peers, who had not been given the opportunity to sit the 11-plus, were in the "B" stream. The hierarchical system of streaming exacerbated the separation of children from different social classes and did little to improve educational opportunities in direct contradiction to the stated aims of government policy. This aligns precisely with the situation described by Reay (2005, p. 298) and again illustrates how progressive educational policies run up against the bedrock of custom, practice, and hegemonic prejudice.

A further example will illustrate how the comprehensive system failed to challenge the notion of who was worthy of a university education. I knew a boy, a few years older than I, who had transferred from the secondary modern to the new comprehensive and therefore carried the label of having failed (or perhaps not taken) the 11-plus. The comprehensive system enabled him to take A-levels, an opportunity that he would have been denied at the old secondary modern. But when he came to apply to university, the school refused to write him a reference until his mother came into school to insist. This boy came from a family of manual workers. His father worked at the local quarry and his mother as a cleaner, and he was clearly deemed unsuitable for a university education despite his academic success at A-level.

Reay writes of the classist attitude to access to higher education and how this permeates not only the ideology of educational professionals. She points out: "the un-acknowledged normality of the middle classes and its corollary, the equally unacknowl-edged pathologisation and diminishing of the working classes" (Reay, 2005, p.911). This hegemonic belief persists among edu-cational professionals despite government policies designed to eradicate such inequalities. Later in my career, I came to see that discrimination on the basis of skin colour or culture persists simi-larly unacknowledged and even denied in the contemporary UK education system.

Encountering misogyny

After school, I worked, saved, and travelled to India to meet the rest of my family. My love of biological sciences brought me back to the United Kingdom to study biochemistry at a prestigious university, and I went on to complete my doctorate in the same discipline.

Growing up as a teenager in the 1970s, I encountered second-wave feminism, and like all my contemporaries at school,

I considered the principle of gender equality to be self-evident. I experienced little by the way of misogyny at school and as an undergraduate, protected in part by my privileged class identity at a good university.

The combative and patriarchal culture of research science became evident to me as a doctoral student. There were many female PhD students but almost no female academic staff in the department. A belief, frequently expressed by the male academics, that women were less capable of rational and conceptual thinking, less worthy of the time and expense of training because of their reproductive capacity, and therefore not serious scientists was deeply undermining. My female peers and I also felt excluded by the male drinking culture, the pub being the site of discussion and exchange of ideas to a large extent.

Once I completed my doctorate, I took up a postdoctoral position in a research institute in Europe, a good step for pursuit of a career in research. However, the move crystallised my growing dissatisfaction with the culture and ways of being in the scientific research community. The competitive, aggressive, and self-aggrandising culture I encountered consolidated my growing sense that I was in the wrong place, and I knew I could not stay in research. I am far from the only woman who left a career in science as a result of the "'macho' culture" and "inappropriate focus on competition" (Society of Biology, 2013).

Thus, my direct experience of a misogynist culture led me to abandon a potentially prestigious research career and move to the margins of the education system as a biology and chemistry lecturer in a small Further Education (FE) college in a deprived London borough.

Working in the margins

The FE college I joined as a junior member of staff was a gloriously diverse institution, in terms of the ethnicities and life experiences of the staff and the students. I recall sitting in the large communal staff room, the hub of the college, and hearing four different languages being spoken around me by my colleagues. Similarly, when teaching chemistry laboratory classes, I would regularly hear at least three languages being used by my students as they conducted their experiments.

This college was truly transformational for me, with a radical ethos towards teaching and learning. I learned so much from my colleagues and from students that has stayed with me throughout my professional career. On reflection, I can see that the inclusive supportive ethos we developed applied to both staff and students. Our practice was cooperative with the focus on supporting students to achieve their full potential. We recognised the multiple disadvantages that they struggled to overcome rather than judging them by their previous educational achievements. It was here I learned first-hand about intersectionality and the ethics of care (Collins, 2000).

The Access movement (Department of Education and Science, 1987) was getting underway when I began my teaching career, and I was soon teaching on and managing an Access in Science course. Access students are adults, largely from low socio-economic groups with few, if any, formal qualifications, with some coming from areas of conflict and persecution as refugees. All were aiming to transform their lives by taking an intense course of study that prepared them for entry to university in a single year. As such, they have a vision and determination that I had not encountered up to this point. Such students represented a challenge to traditional notions of who should go to university.

This was truly working in the margins, recruiting, teaching, and supporting older students who often brought very negative experiences of education with them into my classroom. They challenged my preconceptions and opened me to confront hegemonic assumptions in a way impossible in science research.

In my first year of teaching on the Access programme, one student was a young woman in her late 20s. She had spent many years caring for her mother and was now taking her first steps as an autonomous adult. She was shy, anxious, and had little formal education, having been a school refuser or possibly kept away from school by the demands of her mother. She flourished on the Access course, her confidence growing with every good assignment mark. From someone who wouldn't meet my eye at the start of the course, by the end she sought me out to tell me that she disagreed with the wording of an essay title I had set.

Witnessing at first-hand how education can act like water on a wilting plant was a revelation to me. I come from a middle-class background where class privilege and educational achievement are taken for granted. My fellow students at university had all been confident of success and had either already undergone their transformational experiences or had never, like myself, needed to.

I also came to realise how ill-prepared I was to work in this environment. Another student in the same class came to me and told me how she was receiving free accommodation from her sister in return for helping with childcare but that her sister's partner was sexually harassing her, and she didn't know what to do. I was at a complete loss how to respond as this was something completely beyond my experience. Sara's attendance fell away, and she subsequently left the course. I felt that I had left her down badly by my inexperience and the following year took a course in basic counselling skills. This was transformational for me, and I have drawn on the skills I gained from this throughout my career. Learning to listen without judgement and not to jump in to offer a solution has been extraordinary valuable throughout my professional life. In hindsight, I recognise that I was challenging the normalised "male focused" ways of doing things by adopting this "ethic of care" (Collins, 2000).

Creating change from the margins

Access courses challenged the gatekeepers of the academy. Many Access students did not conform to the normalised model of an undergraduate, 18–19 years old, predominantly White, and middle class. At the time, in the mid-1980s, only around 14 per cent of the population went to university and a further 2–3 per cent attended FE and polytechnical colleges (Bolton, 2012; Maitlis, 1998). Entry to university was by A-level grades, so access to higher education was limited to those students whose families supported them, both financially and culturally, to undertake post-compulsory education.

Access course leaders such as I, pushed at the gates and forced them to open a little wider. We wrote, telephoned, and had meetings with admissions tutors, advocating for our courses and for our students. We challenged admission decisions, sometimes successfully, sometimes not, but with every student who was accepted, the gates were opened a little further.

The students themselves were often pioneers, cutting through the jungle of institutional assumptions and prejudice. A student from the Access course, an Irish man in his late 20s who had worked as a labourer for all his adult life, went for an interview for Geology at Imperial College and a day or so later, the admissions tutor rang me up to discuss how to frame an offer of a place, saying, "have you got any more like him?"

Another student, let's call her Karen, in her early 30s was accepted onto a biology degree programme at King's College, London. She was working class, outspoken, and with strong local accent. She told me that she was in a first-year lecture when the lecturer said, "As you will all know from A level". Karen interrupted him saying, "not everyone here has taken A levels". She described how when the lecturer asked, "How did you get there then?" she had explained the Access course to the whole lecture theatre.

Access courses began to chip away at exclusionary practices as students of other, different origins entered the academy and into graduate professions. Nonetheless, the transition from the nurturing environment of an Access course where a Black feminist, ethic of care (Collins, 2000) was enacted to a much larger institution where normalised assumptions of class, race, and academic literacy prevailed could be challenging. Much as we liked to think we had adequately prepared our students, many experienced shock and trauma as they moved into university study. I recall phone conversations with recently progressed students, attempting to persuade them to give themselves time to adjust to the new culture. In hindsight we forced these students to be involuntary pioneers, sending them to hack their way through the jungle of privilege to enter spaces which were unprepared to receive them. Not all had the confidence to survive, but I stand in awe of the abilities, strengths, and resilience of these students from the margins as they forged their own paths through the academy and society.

Challenging institutional norms from a portacabin in the car park

I eventually passed back through the portals to higher education myself, moving to a relatively high-ranking university to take up a post that combined managing a Foundation Year in Science and Engineering with what became the leadership of a team delivering the university's response to the new Labour government's Widening Participation (WP) strategy. I quickly realised that I had truly moved to the margins of the academy: "To be in the margin is to be part of the whole but outside the main body" (hooks, 1984, p. ix). Wherever WP practitioners got together at conferences or partnership meetings, we shared a joke that WP was implemented from a portacabin in the car park, a temporary construction outside and hidden away from the main academy.

The national WP policy aimed to increase the number of students from disadvantaged backgrounds attending university. It categorised pupils from socio-economic groups under-represented in higher education as lacking aspiration and motivation to aim for university. In my view, this merely articulated the privileged position of those charged with developing such initiatives at national level. The underlying assumption was that students from these "under-represented groups" needed merely to be shown the advantages that a university degree conferred to start putting the necessary effort into their studies. This advantage was often framed only in terms of higher lifetime earnings of graduates (Britton et al., 2020). I imagined White, public school-educated, probably male, policymakers developing the strategy with little or no experience of the people the policy was intended to reach.

For me, this approach positioned the students as the problem rather than addressing the structural racist, classist, and social factors that acted as barriers to academic achievement. From experience, I knew that students from ethnic minorities and their parents from impoverished urban areas are very aware of the advantages of education and certainly did not lack motivation. What they lack is access to good schools, role models, and the social, cultural, and financial capital to thrive academically.

My approach to WP was therefore to use the university resources to enhance local school pupils' academic achievement. We established Saturday schools, revision programmes, and arranged access to the university library as a study space in addition to the aspiration-raising activities required by the WP funding. I felt strongly that it was profoundly unethical to bring local school pupils into the university and subject them to aspiration-raising activities, only to for them to be rejected because their grades were too low. I faced hostility from some staff for bringing "these people" into the university. On one occasion when I was bringing in a group of local school pupils aged around 15–16 for a university "experience", a member of the university expressed concern that they might steal the computers, such was the prevailing attitude to the surrounding community.

I saw the Foundation programme as a major element in WP. The programme was never considered part of the university's programme offer, partly because Foundation students were an eclectic mix of students, predominantly from ethnic minorities who lacked grades for degree entry. I was told a few weeks into the post, "that of course, when recruitment picks up, the Foundation Year will go". This was despite that the progression of Foundation students onto degree programmes sustained undergraduate numbers in more than one academic department in the university. The institutional shame attached to the existence of the Foundation course arose because the university was not able to recruit appropriately qualified applicants to science and engineering disciplines. There was also hostility due to the fear that the low grades and other, unrecognised qualifications of the Foundation students would adversely affect the university's ranking in the national league tables.

An ethic of care and personal accountability

It was here, on my return to a higher education institution, that I encountered an academic culture which did not value students. The cooperative, team approach that my FE colleagues and I found so effective in supporting students was absent, the competitive culture unchanged from my earlier experiences and students regarded an inconvenience. I recall a female academic talking to me about her tutee, a Black Foundation student who suffered from stress. He had come to see her and manifested his anxieties so strongly that she had shouted at him to get out of her office.

The personal accountability I felt towards my students was in direct contrast to the accountability felt by senior staff and managers of the university. My sense was that, to the university management, the success of students was secondary to the reputation of the institution. There was a fear that WP, letting "these people" into the academy, would mean reducing entry requirements and the lowering of academic standards. I argued from my position in the margins that, if the structural barriers to academic achievement could be dismantled, by the additional year of the Foundation programme, for example, academic standards could be maintained, and the university would benefit by an enhanced reputation for social justice and a more diverse student body. However, my vision was not shared, and I left this university after a decade as my role become increasingly untenable. The free market neoliberalism within which higher education is obliged to operate meant that the university's commitment to WP, never wholehearted from the beginning, was becoming increasingly peripheral to its "mission". I did feel I had made a difference in the time I was there; some of the initiatives I developed became established practice. The academic who had said to me ten years earlier that the Foundation Year would soon not be required, expressed regret at my departure, saying, "but who will advocate for the students now?"

An example of decolonisation

My route to the social sciences has involved a major shift in my understanding of knowledge and research methodology. This began with a collaboration with a colleague on a paper on reflexive pedagogy (Burke and Dunn, 2006). Two years later, I was asked to give a talk on Widening Participation Policy and Practice to postgraduate students. This led to an invitation to become the third member of a team developing a master's programme entitled Education, Power, and Social Change.

Putting Black feminist thought into practice

During this time, my colleagues and I put into practice what I now see as enacting Black feminist thought and an example of a decolonising pedagogy. It was an opportunity to bring together my understandings and experiences of the effects of race, class, and gender to explore issues of colonisation, power, educational reproduction, and transformation. As lecturers and tutors, we shared much of ourselves on the programme, using our identities to inform our teaching, building trust as well as the co-creation of knowledge.

Through our teaching, we put into practice several aspects of Patricia Hill Collins's thought through our engagement with intersectionality, the centring of lived experiences and our exploration of hegemonies and the flow of power. We encouraged our students to use Collins's Black epistemological approach in their research projects and enabled them to find their own voices in their writing.

As I reflect upon this programme and my engagement with it over 12 years, as lecturer, personal tutor, module leader, and sometimes as the programme director, I can see that it exemplifies a decolonised programme of study, both in the issues that were addressed, the collegiality and authenticity of experience brought by the core team of staff, and in the way that the students were valued for their experience and insights. From this I have developed the principle of a decolonised pedagogy that is applicable throughout the academy.

Thinking about a decolonising pedagogy

This exercise in reflection and autoethnographic writing has been personally interesting and challenging for me. I go back to the opening statement quoted from bell hooks (1994, p. 2) to reiterate that, until recently, I did not define or articulate my practice as a teacher and educator in theoretical terms and did not see myself able to contribute to the decolonising agenda in higher education. However, as a result of considering my journey from a White-identifying middle-class biochemist to a mixed-race social scientist, I want to propose a concept of a decolonising pedagogy that could be applied across the academy independent of academic discipline.

The challenge of decolonising the academy is complex and ill-defined. Is it changing the curriculum, adding writers of colour to reading lists, introducing diverse positionings and understandings, providing better support to students from minority communities, exposing the colonial links of the academy, or all of these and more? Amending the curriculum will not decolonise science teaching as knowledge is subject to independent verification through experiment, and students are required to apply scientific and mathematical principles to solve problems. Knowing that the name "algebra" derives from a book on the topic by a Persian scholar in the ninth century will not aid students in solving quadratic equations (Al-Khalili, 2010). Moreover, none of these approaches addresses the deep-seated and unarticulated discourse of White privilege within the institution which is at the root of the need for decolonisation.

Academic culture is deeply imbued with colonial attitudes that position anyone outside the normalised group as lesser and of questionable significance. Many university staff, themselves products of unacknowledged privilege, have little understanding of the lived experience of others outside their closed community. I have frequently observed how many staff speak of students in contemptuous terms, particularly those who lack the level of academic literacy expected of a "normal" student. Students tend to be regarded as a nuisance and teaching as a distraction from research. The "normalised" student is one who does not make demands on staff time and can navigate their university journey with little or no help.

To decolonise the academy of racism, classism, and gender bias, the problematising of the "nontraditional" student must be abandoned; indeed, the very concept "nontraditional" needs to be jettisoned. As hooks points out (1994, p. 37), "no education is politically neutral". This applies as much to the choice of how to teach and attitudes towards students as to what to teach.

The starting point for anyone working in an educational context is reflexivity, to recognise and articulate the discourses of prejudice and discrimination that have been encultured into all of us since childhood. Following on from this is the acknowledgement of the equal validity of all lived experience. All of us, not just someone positioned as a student, are more willing to share their thoughts and feelings if we feel that we are recognised and heard. The ability to listen and to be heard is central to building trust and supporting learning.

The concept of students as partners in knowledge creation is a powerful pedagogic tool (Jensen and Bennett, 2015) in developing a decolonised pedagogy. This positions the participants as equals in knowledge and experience. When working with adult students, I have always considered that we are equals; we may be experts in different areas of knowledge, but we always learn from each other. The women on the Access courses knew far more about raising children, and navigating intersectional disadvantages and cultural misogyny than I ever will. I just happened to have a greater knowledge of biological science. Similarly, the young people on the Foundation Year from strict Muslim families knew far more about challenging cultural traditions and beliefs than the staff who taught them.

Not leaving the self behind

Another key element of a decolonised pedagogy is the authenticity of the teaching staff. By this, I mean not merely appropriate academic credentials but the sharing of our own struggles and identities. Through the sharing of our experiences of racism, sexism, and classism, we can disrupt the power structures inherent in education between academic experts and students. I have found that sharing my Anglo-Indian background and stories about my family when teaching about colonialism, built trust and reduced the distance between myself and my students in the subsequent discussions. Similarly, sharing my enthusiasm for biological sciences and the challenges I experienced in understanding concepts motivates students and empowers them to ask for further explanation. We should not underestimate the power of bringing our identities, all of them, into the classroom. I once overheard a student telling a fellow student that he only stayed on the Access course because his tutor (me) rode a motorbike. To paraphrase hooks (1994, pp. 3, 16), it is not possible to leave the self behind at the threshold of the classroom and enter with an objective mind, free of experiences and biases. Sharing our own "lived experience" helps reduce the distance between the teacher and the student and enables both to engage more fully in the learning process (Dovey and Awachie, 2019). We need to be aware of our assumptions to avoid stereotyping and to be able to treat each person as an individual and with respect.

Decolonisation is specifically an act of resistance to structural racism, since the notion of White superiority is a direct consequence of colonisation. The positioning of subject peoples as lesser and inferior, is a necessary consequence of colonisation. Universities have reflected and maintained this discourse of privilege, selecting, and training the privileged few to uphold and reproduce the existing structures of power (Ahmed, 2021; Bhopal, 2018; Collins, 2000). There is another discussion to be had here around the difficulties of calling out racism and racist behaviour that is beyond the scope of this chapter. A decolonising pedagogy does, however, provide us with a tool to start the conversation.

Foregrounding personal stories to decolonise the curriculum

Sara Ahmed in her recent book (2021) documents the response to and the outcome of complaints in the academy, the closing of ranks, the shutting of doors to any issue that might challenge the prevailing discourse. A master's student, employed in a UK university, in a dissertation I was privileged to supervise, used her own experience of the institutional response to her complaint of racial harassment by her manager as the basis of her research. She wrote powerfully of how "the university was able to promote equality and diversity without acknowledging racism" (Anya, 2020, p. 17). She discussed White frailty, how the distress of the manager against whom the complaint was directed was used to diminish the severity of the complaint of racism. Structural racism is as present in the academy as in all institutions, but is perhaps especially problematic in higher education where liberal values and critical thinking are celebrated and inform the narrative that the academy tells of itself.

A decolonising pedagogy based on Black feminist principles of lived experience, and an ethic of care can enable deeper changes to the curriculum, across the whole academy. It calls for every individual in the academy to acknowledge and address the assumptions they may carry from their upbringing. Teachers need to foreground their personal stories and expose their vulnerabilities in order to deconstruct the distance between them and their students (Dovey and Awachie, 2019). However, as my own experience shows, progressive proposals designed to promote greater equality in education often come up against hegemonies.

The reluctance of staff to confront their unconscious prejudices will be one example of a hegemonic barrier. Additionally, the prevailing neoliberal, market-driven environment under which universities are obliged to operate, has resulted in a focus on credentialism and targets. Black feminist theory offers us hope against the competition for limited resources and support for the commitment to individualistic personal development afforded by a decolonised pedagogy.

Through discussions of my own lived experience, I have sought to share good practice in thinking about the nature of supporting student learning in higher education. I have considered identity and how Black feminist theory in the work of hooks (1999) has influenced my approaches and has helped me reflect on my own identity in the context of my "lived experience". This chapter demonstrated how lived experience, and reflection can develop an understanding of intersectionality and discrimination, regardless of the privileged, elitist background of the individual in education. As part of this personal narrative, I illustrate two examples of how a pedagogy based on acknowledging and valuing the identities and experiences of both students and tutors can be effective in challenging hegemonic principles and decolonising the academy. Building on this, I propose a decolonising pedagogy that draws on key features of Black feminist thought, particularly an ethic of care, valuing of the identity and critical analysis of unacknowledged hegemonic biases.

The next chapter returns to the theme of class and race as it depicts White working-class identity in decolonising arts-based practice in higher education. The author draws on her deep engagement with Black feminist text to demonstrate its significance and usefulness as a critical tool in decolonising curriculum agenda in higher education.

Learning objective

Critically evaluate the role of decolonising pedagogy in challenging intersectional discrimination in the neoliberal university

4

Conversations that change the decolonising world

Exploring class, disability, and race perspectives in decolonising arts-based feminist research

Beverley Hayward

In the West's unrelenting need to chase the "fast buck", this overt capitalist agenda (Singh, 2018, p. 337) makes it increasingly difficult to practise a pedagogy that considers the ethical foundations which underpin the student journey. This holistic approach draws upon bell hooks's (1994) conceptualisation of education where the needs of students are more than ensuring they gain a qualification, rather than using education as a business to make money in a neoliberal context. Therefore, opening access and widening participation come with moral and ethical considerations that cannot be overlooked. However, to do "justice" to the social, cultural, and well-being needs of the student body, a decolonial approach demands that the university and the curriculum represent those marginalised groups. However, representation must be undertaken in a meaningful way; otherwise, it becomes a form of tokenism. In this constrained managerial strategy advocated in higher education, forgotten are the safe physical and psychological spaces that yearn for the imaginary, for meditation, and for play. For these spaces of creativity to grow, it is necessary for the educator-practitioner to listen to the student body, to hear what they have to say. In communities of creative practice, the power of conversation facilitates change. By bringing together our shared lived experiences and cultures into the academy's classrooms, disadvantaged students, the working class, the neurodiverse, people of colour, and women can see possibilities of hope.

Hope is to be found in a Black feminist-womanist (Etienne, 2016; hooks, 1984) approaches to knowledge production, that embodies an ethic of care, welfarism, and empathy. These conversations of care are to be found in small spaces in higher education that resist the marketisation of education. Values that reproduce the same old Eurocentric masculine practices in education and arts-based research are not of value in our new world. What is of value is engagement in conversations of social justice, activism, and artworks that change the world, and challenge the status quo that repeats patriarchal and colonised discourses.

Introduction

This chapter seeks to explore class and race perspectives in arts-based feminist research and pedagogic practices with an ethic of care, by drawing upon the voices of the marginalised in conversations with the author. This takes the form of vignettes, I-poems, and artwork to document the lived experiences of what Clover (2010) calls "artists as educators" and researchers. To record the embodiment of our resilience in the face of power-knowledges that seek to maintain the old system, practitioners must expose their vulnerabilities, be self-aware, accountable, and authentic. The intersections of race, class, gender, and disability that position the researcher on the margins are spaces from which transformative practices can develop. Those practitioners, once students themselves, were positioned as what Reay calls the "inferior other" (Lewis, 2017). Yet this subjectivity, situated in spaces of resistance, can support change and create transformation. However, those conversations between the student and the educator, and the researched and the researcher must be written, read, heard, and disseminated in the world of academia for change to take place. Being silent, invisible is not going to move society to transform (Lewis, 2017). An example of what I have termed an empathy conversation matrix was created to illustrate how to decolonise higher education practices and engage in dialogue with students and colleagues. The conversations that are documented in this chapter begin in that controversial space of the university library. Here the support worker, Carole Hatfield, discusses the power-knowledge hierarchies that build upon the logic of the Enlightenment and how she destabilises that bastion of knowledge possession by Black feminist art-based practices. The chapter ends in another space of contention, the gallery, where the labours of feminist art-based practices are celebrated.

Part 1: Habitual Currents

In my head, I heard the teacher:
Over and over, over and over,
YOU can't go to uni!
You're too stupid!
Stand behind your chair.
Repeat after me:
You'll be lucky to get ungraded.
Repeat after me:
You are thick,
Repeat after me:
You are stupid.
You can't be an auctioneer,
You are a girl,
You have a cockney accent.

Do you know what I think I am missing?
The ambition gene.
Careers advice?
I would say was a bit poor on the ground.
I remember that there was a table with leaflets.
There were a few:
I would say nursing,
There were the banks,
There was insurance,
And teaching.
I really wanted to go to arts school,

But all the leaflets,
Were pretty gendered really.
She is capable of more than that –
Make her go and do something else,
And she can draw in her spare time.

(Hayward, et al., 2022).

Introducing those in conversation, bell hooks and the research participants

Like bell hooks (1994, p. 3), I never imagined that I would become a teacher. I wanted to be an auctioneer of art and antiques, and she a writer and artist. However, many women, people of colour, of the working class, and those with a disability were and are excluded from careers of their choice. I acknowledge my White privilege, but still, my education as a working-class woman with dyslexia was painful and humiliating. My experiences at school, and to a lesser degree university, were neither supportive nor compassionate. This is voiced in the first verse of the poem "Habitual Currents Part 1" (2022). I deeply felt the pain of marginalisation, as did hooks. Her "teachers derive their primary pleasure in the classroom by exercising their authoritarian power over fellow students, crushing our spirits, and dehumanising our minds and bodies" (hooks, 1994, p. 2). Similar experiences were told to me by a group of working-class White women: our voices formed the co-constructed poems presented in this chapter. My voice is the first verse and Carole Hatfield the rest. Our conversations explore the complexities of the role in which we began to see ourselves as "artist as educator" in higher education. As we conversed, I got to know this resilient cohort of women through many emotional conversations; I was intrigued to understand their lived experiences.

Understanding the importance of empathetic conversations was the beginning of a research and teaching tool, a conversation matrix, which I now share. We discussed how we felt, behaved, and saw ourselves, as artists, mothers, students, and support workers; what we know and how we know it; the barriers and motivations to learning and becoming artists. The basic conversation matrix was created by me in a visual format, to understand the intersectionality of my research, to support a caring, empathetic, and ethical approach to research, teaching, and understanding positionality, an example of which is presented latterly in the chapter as to how we might converse ethically in higher education.

Initially, the conversations for the poems were gathered for my PhD study (Hayward, 2019) and the poems accompanied an art exhibition in 2022, entitled *Unruly Women*. In this visual and celebratory presence, we were neither silent nor absent; our bodies were seen and in "coming to voice", the oppressed were heard (hooks, 1994, p. 185; Freire, 1970). The poems, the art, and the exhibition, Figure 1, illuminated the practice of our art and craft in the everyday, contextualising the subject positions of the artist-educator, meaning maker, and knowledge creator. More importantly, the voices in the stories explain the need for teaching to be caring and empathetic, as "healer" and "mentor" (hooks, 1994, p. 14).

The classroom should be "fun" (Lane, in Hayward, et al., 2022), "an exciting place, never boring" (hooks 1994, p. 7): a space in which all can contribute, not a Gradgrindian lesson of filling up with facts, to "learn obedience to authority" (hooks, 1994, pp. 4, 203). Therefore, we used our experiences to facilitate "a legacy of care" and encouragement, as educators, artists, and researchers (Hayward, 2014). We need to be open to feminist art practices, pedagogies, and research. This approach enables authentic, ethical protocols and embodied praxis (hooks, 1994, p. 54; Smith, 1999, p. 4). To teach, research, write, and curate differently, with integrity, authenticity, and vulnerability, enables the oppressed voices of research participants and students to be heard. Searching for new knowledges, as a White neurodiverse feminist, I explore what it means to be an embodied, unruly, reflexive practitioner in the "order" of the academy. Seeking to explore the intersection of disability, class, and race perspectives in arts-based feminist research and pedagogic practices (Massey, 1996), I draw upon the voices of support workers in conversation me, with each other, *and with bell hooks*. The spaces of the classroom, the library, and galleries are used as a backdrop to illustrate the power of feminist arts-based practice, poetry, storytelling, and textiles. In conversations and practice, we reframe the functionality and purpose of spaces to address injustices. The chapter shows the power of conversations, taking the form of vignettes, data poems, and the exhibition to document our experiences of what Clover (2010) calls "artists as educators" and researchers. The theoretical context is guided by bell hooks's care and compassionate ethos in higher education (hooks, 1994, p. 86).

Figure 1 *Unruly Women*, 2022, at the Nucleus Gallery Chatham, Kent.

Photograph by Beverley Hayward, from left to right, featuring the work of Beverley Hayward, Jackie Hagan, Carole Hatfield, Chrissie Peters, Vickie Lane, and Luna Zsigo.

Conversations in context

Indeed, the support worker role, a caring and empathetic position, was taken up after our job of choice was eliminated as an option by those wielding that authoritarian power. During an interview conducted on 6 June 2016, Carole Hatfield described how the Catholic nuns decided that art was not a career for her, much the same as bell hooks's parents: "To them art was play. It was not something real – not a way to make a living. To them I was not a talented artist" (hooks, 1995, p. 2). To put our conversations into context: we did not go to university from school, but as first-generation, mature students, I joined the Open University, and the participants joined The University for the Creative Arts (UCA). We had no study skills. We could neither write an essay nor do research, so the same might be said of some students that enrol on courses, many of whom we supported. We lacked the confidence that privilege brings. However, eventually, we learned how to read the rules of "the old game" (Cixous, 1976, p. 880).

Once in the game, we saw for ourselves the limitations that were placed upon marginalised students. We worked in the disability department at UCA, and it is from this landscape that I share our stories. For a time, we did hold onto the outcast, imposter, inter-loper subjectivity (Bourdieu and Champagne, 1999; hooks, 1994; Reay, 2004; Reay et al., 2010), unable to escape the patriarchal Eurocentric discourses inscribed on our bodies. "Poverty of ambi-tion" was embedded in our psyche (Saunders, 2009) through the "habitual currents" of gender, race, and class discourses that oppressed a creative identity (Hayward, 2019; Woolf, 1927). However, just as power disables, so does it enable (Foucault, 1978, p. 95), where resistance, resilience, and activism are possi-ble (hooks, 1994). My research and the support workers' practices as artists-educators illustrate this. I created *Sewing Sampler: Home Is Where the Art Is*, as a reminder of the challenges we faced in the pursuit of dreams of becoming artists. Often, we conversed about our art, created with portable inexpensive materials, as there was a scarcity of time, money, and space. Housework and artwork merged. The kitchen-dining table facilitated creative possibilities of agency in the political and personal.

Not only are their resistances to oppression voiced and visual-ised in their art, but so too is a hooksian commitment to inclu-sive pedagogies, which are voiced in *Part 2* of the poem "Flying Above and Beyond" (2022):

> I now consider myself to be an artist.
> I feel it has helped me inspire young people,
> To achieve their dream and be creative.
> I want to inspire people,
> To not stop being creative.

So, if they are in an art's uni,
Like they are not there for nothing.
It doesn't matter what they do with art,
As long as they recognise,
That they are creative,
As I am creative,
I can encourage.
I liked ceramics.

I liked the woodwork.
And I like making anything,
I've never really settled,
I'm a multimedia artist.
I am an artist.
Helping people.
Well, if anyone's in need,
Then I seem to be there,
At the right time.
So, if I can help,
In any way,
To get them through,
To the next stage,
Even in the background.
You know, I think,
Art should be fun.

In conversation with bell hooks

It is now nearly 30 years on since hooks wrote her influential book *Teaching to Transgress* (1994), and 20 years since I read it as a student teacher. Unfortunately, as Singh (2018) points out, in the West's unrelenting need to chase the "quick buck", this

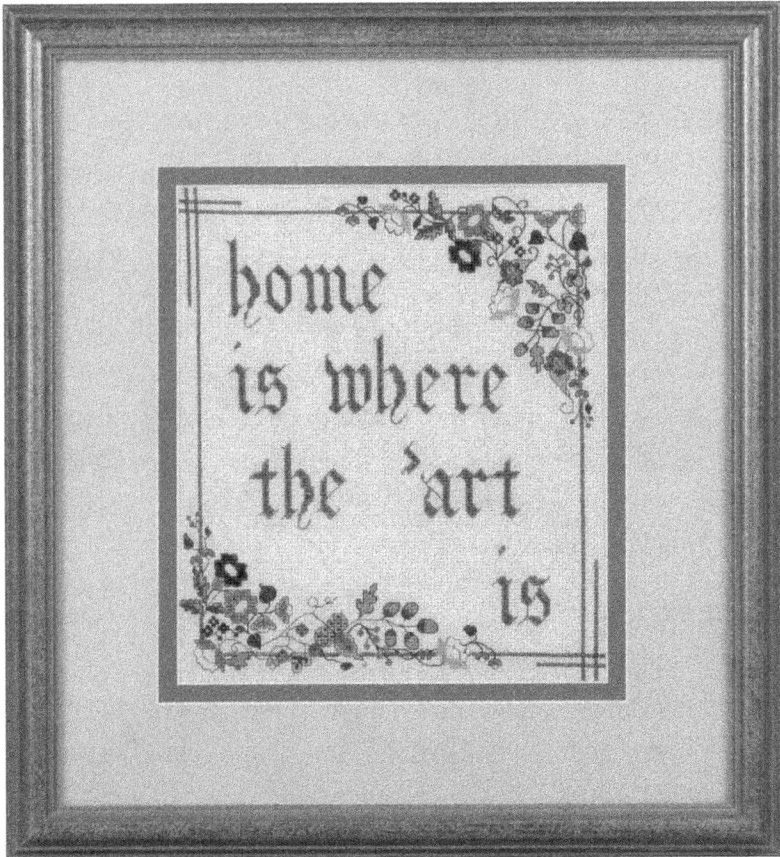

Figure 2 Beverley Hayward, *Sewing Sampler: Home Is Where the Art Is,* 2014, tapestry, private collection (photographed by Rob Roach).

overt neoliberal agenda makes it increasingly difficult to practise a pedagogy that considers the ethical foundations which
underpin the student and/or research journey. Harvey (2007)
states that neoliberalism is "[a] political project to re-establish the
conditions for capital accumulation and to restore the power of
economic elites" (p. 19). He continues: "neoliberalism was from
the very beginning an endeavour to restore class power to the
richest strata in the population" (p. 28). Often, pedagogic and
research practices have fallen foul of unethical procedures (Ball,

2013; Lygo-Baker et al., 2019) as research is neither "innocent" nor a "distant academic exercise" (Smith, 1999, p. 5). Accordingly, universities must: "create organisations where everyone can flourish irrespective of skin, colour, gender, sexual orientation, religion" (Beavan, 2020, p. 104). Unfortunately, as practitioners we are still facing the same issues that hooks observed many years ago:

> As backlash swells, as budgets are cut, as jobs become even more scarce, many of the few progressive interventions that were made to change the academy, to create an open climate for cultural diversity are in danger of being undermined or eliminated. These threats should not be ignored. (hooks, 1994, p. 33)

We certainly felt the effects of the backlash. Discrimination is pervasive: we were considered neither artists nor academics, but rather an embodiment of patriarchy's othering of us (Beatty, 2007; Parker and Pollock, 1981). We, working-class female support workers, were in our place. Situated in student services, we came under the label of "helper", from the "mum's army" (Stevens, 2013), invading spaces on the margins of academia (hooks, 1984; Puwar, 2004). Nevertheless, there are those of us who fight on, with bell hooks as a source of inspiration. Since reading her work as a mature student teacher, I conversed with her every day. She was the only theorist out of the plethora of dead White men to whom I could relate. I laminated her words and stuck them to my computer screen in the form of small starbursts. Her voice was inspiring:

> To educate as the practice of freedom is a way of teaching that anyone can learn. That learning process comes easiest to those of us who can teach who also believe that there is an aspect of our vocation that is sacred; who

believe that our work is not merely to share information but to share in the intellectual and spiritual growth of our students. (hooks, 1994, p. 13)

With her passing in 2022, I felt the need to pay homage to this working-class woman of colour who guided me on my journey. Her holistic approach draws upon a conceptualisation of education where the individual student need is more than ensuring a qualification is acquired. Accordingly, opening access and widening participation come with moral and ethical considerations that cannot be overlooked. The university is a site of political and cultural knowledge production and dissemination, and as such, a site of danger for many. Bhambra et al. (2018) observe: "[i]t was in the university that colonial intellectuals developed theories of racism, populated discourses that bolstered support for colonial endeavours and provided ethical and intellectual grounds for the dispossession, oppression and domination of colonised subjects" (p. 5). Here racism, sexism, and elitism were promoted and continually reproduced in classrooms and research. Research is the product that fills books to be placed in libraries and therefore, as writers, we have a responsibility. For in writing as a method of knowing, I was conscious of, and reflective upon, the research process. Denzin and Lincoln (2005) state, "[s]adly, qualitative research, in many if not all of its forms (observation, participation, interviewing, ethnography), serves as a metaphor for colonial knowledge, for power, and for truth" (p. 1). The "knowledgeable" ethnographer embedded in the superiority of colonialist anthropologies was a position I was conscious to avoid (Spivak, 1988). Ethical research facilitates "a reclamation of (ab)original ways of transferring knowledge and troubles hegemonic systems of education" (Bhambra et al, 2018, p. 9).

In this way, a feminist decolonial approach demands that the university, the curriculum, research, and art represent those marginalised groups, but in doing so the social, cultural, and well-being needs of the student body, participants, and researcher must be considered in the "care of the soul" (hooks, 1994, p. 16). And so, representation in the academy and research must be undertaken in a meaningful way; otherwise, it becomes a form of tokenism (hooks, 1994, p. 39). Unfortunately, in a constrained managerial strategy, advocated in higher education, forgotten are the physical and psychological community spaces that yearn for creative ways of knowing. Nevertheless, they exist in pockets of universities and galleries. Art-based methods of experimentation, meditation, and play flourish in what I call the *Feminist Imaginary*, as this chapter demonstrates (Clover et al., 2022; hooks, 1994, p. 61).

Feminist arts-based research

It was these tensions and social complexities, specifically the political nature of education and the artworld that my research sought to illuminate. And in doing so, the use of arts-based research and teaching methods can be used as an example for the readers of this book and the student researchers I have the privilege to teach. This is a physical and visible resistance to the dominant ideologies of Eurocentric heteronormative practices. From the novice compliant researcher (Collins and Cooper, 2014), struggling to find my voice, to exploring different methodological approaches (Denzin and Lincoln, 2005; Owton, 2017;

Richardson, 1997), I can embrace the personal and political. I address the inequalities and pain of discrimination to produce new power and knowledges. These injustices were at the core of my consciousness and motivated my research, and therefore I urge my students to research and write about what motivates them in a political act of documentation (hooks, 1994). So, like many of my students, I knew what I wanted to research, but not how to research. It is Smith (1999) and hooks (1994) from whom I sought guidance to understand Black feminist pedagogies and art-based practices. Research and teaching are a sharing of the process, a sharing of knowledges, inclusion, and collaboration. In these practices I hope to become an effective searcher for new knowledges of value, by encouraging the narratives as they are gifted to me (Cixous, 1975; Scheurick and Young, 1997).

Conversations to change the world

For these practices of creativity to grow, it is necessary for the educator-practitioner to listen to the student body and the researched, to hear what they have to say. In communities of imaginary creative practice (Clover et al., 2022; hooks, 1995; Wenger, 1998), the power of conversations facilitates change. By bringing together our shared experiences and cultures into the academy's classrooms, those disadvantaged students, members of the working class, neurodiverse people, people of colour, and women can see possibilities of hope (Clover et al., 2022). Using hooks's approach to "progressive", "holistic" education is how I try to teach and undertake research, the emphasis being on care of the self and others (hooks, 1994, p. 15). The inclusion of creative approaches is a way in which to resist dominant discourses and those subject positions that are often populated by authority figures, the curator, the artist, the educator, and the researcher. These approaches are encouraged by breaking away from the constraints of traditional academic writing: "It avoids the ('masculine') impulse to appropriate or annihilate the other's difference, allowing the other to remain as 'other'" (Blythe and Sellers, 2004, p. 15), and thereby situates students and the researched as active, resilient, speaking subjects (Lather, 2000).

So, what does the practice of feminist arts-based approaches look like? Those new to writing and researching "academically differently" (Jackson, 2004) try playing with poetry and art-craft methods (hooks, 1984, p. 2; Hoult et al., 2020). Often in the academy methodologies and approaches are abstract concepts that are slippery, lacking contextualisation and relevance to the marginalised (hooks, 1994, p. 19); again, this is another way in which to exclude those who are not in "the know". This is the way of catalogued, ordered masculine economies of knowledge found in the library, divorcing theory from practice. Tomes of theories and concepts are laid to rest, yet still discussed in lectures. These theories are rarely connected to practical examples or lived experiences by the authors who write about them. The library becomes the place where students go to uncover these well-guarded secrets, where the power and knowledge of the "masters" are visibly stored, awaiting students to "possess" them. (Cixous, 1975, pp. 136–160). The space is a physical reminder of the valued visible knowledges to be found in the academy, a legacy of the Enlightened Eurocentric *The Order of Things* (Foucault, 1970). It is a library of art history that privileges the canon of

European White men (Parker and Pollock, 1981). The spaces pay homage to those who have little relevance or context to many students in the twenty-first century, and thereby exclude the yet-to-be-written and published, valued-less knowledges the support workers are producing. Those knowledges are embedded in ethical practices of care, community, and collaboration. They are examples of effective pedagogies and creative ways to decolonise the curriculum, the university, and art practices.

For example, Hatfield encourages her students to be inspired and, indeed, motivated to research. She expounds upon imaginative ways books are used in the library, by practising art-based methods. We subvert and resist the norms of the library's function by making the space fun and exciting, a space of play and conversation, daring to talk rather than bestow reverence on White men of privilege. As support workers, we stave off "the overwhelming boredom, uninterest, and apathy" in the classroom (hooks, 1994, p. 10). Hatfield informs me:

> every time you get a new student, in your first session: "actually we are not going to be doing any writing today, we are going into the library and walk round". I show them the wonders, the pleasures of looking down a row and just picking a random book and opening it up and thinking what will I find here? [...] it is to get them enthusiastic about using books and just opening a book. [...] which none of our lot are doing. Then they think: "what am I going to make? I don't know, what am I interested in?".
>
> They are like the rabbit in the headlights; decide that you are going to walk up and down every row and every

so often take a book out randomly, just for the hell of it.
And bit by bit you might find one idea, you might think
I'm going to follow this one. (Hatfield, 2019)

Hatfield (2019) discusses the complexities of this space, and how important the library, books, and research are: "If I'm really honest, […] one of the reasons for staying is to work in the university so that I can have good access to the library". The space of the library facilitates their position – artist as educator and researcher. Hatfield's use of this space subverts the norms of research as encouraged by the academy.

In every case, the students are given a brief to explore. A reading list is included which has the texts for the usual categories of visual cultures pertinent to the topic. In Hatfield's practice, the brief is ignored for an unusual journey of discovery in a random unconventional use of books. The students are encouraged to ignore the assignment brief in favour of starting to discover, by chance, information that might be drawn upon in the research stage of a project. This unusual use of the library is a way to explore knowledge visually because research for these students is often alien and an activity that causes anxiety and distress. For many students, it is an extremely stressful space, where failure around literacy is brought to the fore. This, the support workers are aware of, and some have experienced very negative learning experiences themselves. Research in the library can be intimidating, restricting, and perpetuating systemic inequality, not dissimilar to Hatfield's own experience as a student:

I remember reading something in the schoolbooks that
I thought was a bit racist when I was about 16 and so I
went into the local library to look it up, and the librarian

nearly boxed my ears. She said that's not for a school-girl in a uniform, that's for the over-18s. "Get out now". But I said that it was in my history book. I've only come to look it up. "I know your sort. Get out". They were very puritanical. (Hatfield, 2019)

Thus, situated in reproducing negative practices, knowledges can be restricted by gatekeepers. To borrow from hooks (1994), "it takes a fierce commitment, a will to struggle, to let our work as teachers reflect progressive pedagogies" (p. 143). From our experiences, we sought to facilitate learning that was fun, playful, experimental. There were conversations to be had in an ethic of care. I hoped that the curriculum, now five years on in 2022, was more inclusive, so I sourced the assignment brief for media. The cover depicted three images by European White men with naked White female muses. Disheartened? Yes. Surprised, no! hooks (1994) made the same point nearly 30 years ago: "We inhabit real institutions where very little seems to be changed, where there are very few changes in the curriculum, almost no paradigm shifts, and where knowledge and information continue to be presented in the conventionally accepted manner" (p. 143).

I decided to try out Hatfield's research technique in the library to find artists of colour who might be researched for the brief. I walked up and down the stalls, to no avail, their voices could not be heard. I "cheated", by using the library catalogue, setting the filters to Rochester campus and "Black artist". I only got 116 hits. The books were sandwiched between feminist art theory and cultural theory after "Chaves". Accordingly, if I could not find these books easily, how would students fare with limited experience of searching in this space? However, we cannot give up.

We must take up a subjectivity that challenges the "machinery's functioning" (Cixous, 1975, p. 65). The artist as educator has a responsibility to those students who search in libraries to hear their opinions and see themselves represented in research, books on shelves, galleries, and museums. But more importantly, the stories should be told by those who are doing the telling, not the "expert" academic. Feminist arts-based practices encourage conversations using new technology, and conversation can be international via online platforms.

As well as presenting our work in exhibitions, other ways to try to redress these inequalities, as Smith (1999) discusses, are to have our collective voice heard through conferences, papers, and relevant books. Our art and practices embody experiences and emotions of the day-to-day, the past, and the present, immersed in spirituality, mystery, and catharsis. The practices must disrupt the totalising mastery discourses, to subvert the status quo (hooks, 1994, p. 172; 1995, p. 105) via the intersections of race, class, gender, and disability which may reposition the researcher-practitioner in spaces outside the academy. Figure 3 celebrates that destabilisation in queering the gender and race of a child, the illustration of which is layered upon the textiles of the Empire. I travelled with Chrissie as the conceptualisation of the artwork took shape and we conversed to notice and acknowledge the silencing of the self and Others.

Conversations using an ethical caring matrix

As practitioners, once students, we are residing in spaces outside those institutions (hooks, 1994, p. 30), where conversation can be had and heard. Those conversations help to right some of the injustices that marginalised groups endure. "Unthinking mastery" discourses are required to change the world (Singh, 2018), and by doing so, what does it mean to navigate my position as a feminist arts-based researcher, for that was what I was to become? One way to achieve this is through the creation of data poems. This I did by using a storytelling approach to support an understanding of and care for the research participant. This technique can be adapted using an empathic and ethical Q & A matrix for students, and it is also a useful tool to be reflexive upon the intersectionality of the researcher.

Figure 3 Beverley Hayward and Chrissie Peters, Travelling in a Cosmopolitan Milieu, 2022, embroidered collage with paper and acetate (photographed by Rob Roach).

For this chapter, I have used the matrix to foster inclusive, decolonised, active learning that both the tutor and the student can explore. It supports an understanding of contextualised relatable learning. By actively listening to the student, tutors can understand not only what motivates and stimulates learning, but also it is a method to explore the individual barriers to learning. The conversations can be ongoing in personal tutorials, as group exercises, or undertaken discreetly. To be explored are the intersectionality of the learner, how they see themselves, their behaviours, feelings, beliefs, barriers, and motivations to learn.

Conversation matrix

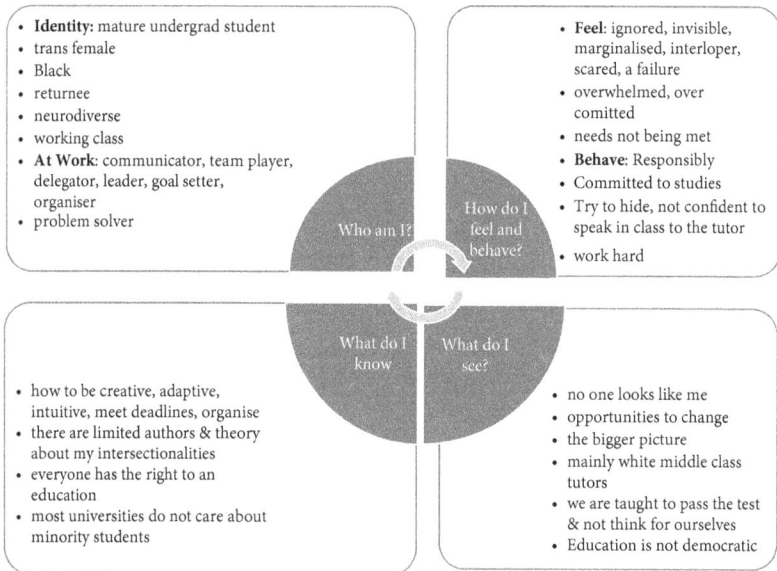

Who am I?
- **Identity:** mature undergrad student
- trans female
- Black
- returnee
- neurodiverse
- working class
- **At Work:** communicator, team player, delegator, leader, goal setter, organiser
- problem solver

How do I feel and behave?
- **Feel:** ignored, invisible, marginalised, interloper, scared, a failure
- overwhelmed, over comitted
- needs not being met
- **Behave:** Responsibly
- Committed to studies
- Try to hide, not confident to speak in class to the tutor
- work hard

What do I know
- how to be creative, adaptive, intuitive, meet deadlines, organise
- there are limited authors & theory about my intersectionalities
- everyone has the right to an education
- most universities do not care about minority students

What do I see?
- no one looks like me
- opportunities to change
- the bigger picture
- mainly white middle class tutors
- we are taught to pass the test & not think for ourselves
- Education is not democratic

The matrix explores who we are, what we feel, how we are seen and heard and by whom. Therefore, it is important to have a physical presence, as the following conversations illustrate. It is true what Marian Wright Edelman, founder and president of the

Children's Defense Fund, said, "You can't be what you can't see". Being seen at the exhibition provoked many powerful emotions and conversations, embodying the *Unruly Women*, as artists creating, writing, and curating disorder. We understood our exclusion by "an art world so rooted in the politics of white-supremacist capitalist patriarchy" (hooks, 1995, p. xii). This made the statement by Vicky Lane, an artist and participant, particularly compelling: "I actually feel like a real artist, now I have exhibited in a real gallery". Below is a photograph of the exhibition in situ.

Powerful too was a statement from a current international master's student of colour. She said the poem above "should be used as a teaching tool", as this was how she felt when she entered the academy. Thus, our "small stories" are told as a celebration of our achievements (Georgakopoulou, 2015). To borrow from hooks (1995), art is political and our conversations in the academy needed airing to show what is possible for those who follow: "[w]e make spaces for dialogue across boundaries, we engage a process of cultural transformation that will ultimately create a revolution in vision" (xvi). Arts-based research serves as a meaningful approach to achieve these aims. It is a powerful medium because the images it generates remain alive in the psyche of the individual, resonating deeply. As bell hooks explains, "materials have memories" (hooks, 1995, p. 22). Our exhibition illustrates defiance of the masters' misdeeds of exclusion and oppression. Our voices are heard in the words of participant poetry, and in our deeds, the art-craftwork on display. These political acts of resilience, rebellion, and activism address the lack of participant voice in the field of poetic inquiry used as a curatorial tool to caption and accompany art exhibitions. Furthermore, to capture the shared nature of our "passion of experience" (hooks, 1994, p. 89), the data poems are themed to gather our collective voices.

Stenhouse (2014) warns against a collective approach as it loses the individuality of the experience. However, the spirit of my research was to bring a group of *Unruly Women* together to communicate a collective identity. As Lather (2000) suggests, the ethnographer "offers or facilitates the voice of the researched and the researcher toward more 'authentic' knowing" (p. 17). Our experiences, lives, and practices were group-orientated as entanglements. Accordingly, the exhibition was a collaboration of collective negotiations. Decisions were made on what to display, spacing, placement of work, and staffing of the exhibition. I set up a WhatsApp group so that every step of the way, I could seek advice from the exhibitors. I contacted each one about the construction of the data poem and asked for their consent and what they would like to have in the poem exhibited. They all said, "we trust you, Bev, you pick the text". This was a huge privilege of co-construction, having the responsibility of representation. Before the *Unruly Women* (2022) exhibition, I wrote the blurb. But to write differently, I needed to resist authoritative moves. I discarded the blurb and opened the exhibition with a poem. But more importantly, I closed the exhibition with *Habitual Currents* and *Flying Above and Beyond*. I wanted the visitors to leave with our poems and *Art on [their] Mind* (hooks, 1995).

Hoult (2012a, 2012b, 2020), Richardson (1997), and MacLure, (2011) state that writing and researching differently resist those authoritative moves I discussed using the writings of bell hooks. So how fortuitous it was that I had a vast data source upon which to draw, to exhibit poetry as well as their art to contest the rigidity and logic of mastery structures of writing and exhibiting (MacLure, 2011). As far as I am aware, transcription poetry or participant voice poetry has not been used to accompany an art-craft exhibition. Grounded in feminist theory and rigor, art-based practice makes an innovative contribution to new knowledges. Although it is in its infancy, my work is closely aligned with that of Patricia Leavy (2008), who uses poems to engage with an art installation. Like her, I turn to a style that accords openness and experimentation, to create a new, different "body" of work.

The feminist researcher's reflections upon art-based practices

Feminist art-based practices are an approach to seeing different realities, whatever sex, gender, race, or religion. Thus, as writing, knowledges, spaces, and conversations are social constructs, they can be deconstructed. It is possible to disrupt the power and knowledge hierarchies that dominate those about whom we write, those who do the writing, and how we write and research (Richardson in Denzin and Lincoln, 2005, p. 962). In feminist ways of knowing, they foster a sensitivity on the part of the researcher to those researched (Bloor, 2001, p. 392; Oakley 1981), and on the part of the teacher to those learning. Thereby spaces are created for the telling of stories. I take on the role of what West (2016) suggests is the "sympathetic other" [...] in a "supportive relationship all of which requires an imaginative empathetic, reflexive engagement" (p. 36). Thus, it is to understand the production of the feminist researcher and the researched as subjects in a relationship that embodies negotiated decisions and dialogue. Our researcher and curatorial subjectivities are formed in an ethic of care and community (hooks, 1994), shaped by relationality, inter-dependence, and collaboration. This formation negates individualism, neoliberalism, and masculinised discourses. Our bodies as researcher-researched, student-educator make their way to meet each other in a community of the imaginary. In this creative space the perspectives of others can be heard and imagined "listened to" and "taken seriously" (West, 2016, p. 38).

In this way of researching and teaching, now neither silent nor invisible, we create our story by speaking and hearing, by the practice of poetry and storytelling, as a "healing tool" (Bainbridge et al., 2021). In conjunction with the exhibition of our art, researching and writing differently is a form of disorder, an active resistance to galvanise change. We are not units to be counted in and out of the academy, as are the books in the library by the keepers of knowledge; rather, we are self-aware practitioners, exposing our vulnerabilities and taking "care of the soul" (hooks, 1994). In a feminist-womanist ontological lens (Etienne, 2016), care and welfarism are a necessity. We must take care of the self, ourselves, colleagues, students, and the researched. Thereby, as a community, we resist the marketisation of education, research, and curation.

We resist those habitual norms in the functioning of briefs, libraries, galleries, and museums that seek to represent all but *us*. Those conversations between the student and educator, and the researched and researcher must be written, read, heard, and disseminated in the world for change to occur. Thus, a new game must be played; new conversations must be had. Values that reproduce the same old Eurocentric masculine practices in education and arts-based research are not of value in our new world. What is of value is engagement in conversations of social justice and activism to challenge the repetition of patriarchal and colonised discourses. In our exhibitions "radical possibility" prevails, where alternative discourses are found "not just in words but in the habits of being" (hooks 1989, p. 20). Those habits include documenting feminist art-based practices and new exciting visual cultures.

Thus, to return to the data poem I used to open this chapter and to close the exhibition, it does describe our struggles, but so does it illuminate our successes and how we sought a different way to practise our craft as artists as educators. For this chapter, it is an example of what an application of feminist arts-based practice and research might look like to those researchers and students seeking an inclusive method. For those schooled in extractivist, objectifying, positive methods, different methodologies are available (Spivak, 1988): these include authentic storytelling through conversation, poetry, and art-craft, which prioritize collaboration and shared experiences. Exhibitions are a platform from where all can be present, seen as artists, creators of new knowledges, as educating and having our own conversations so that "if art moves us – touches our spirit – it is not easily forgotten" (hooks, 1995, p. 35). It is a way to provoke difficult and painful conversations to develop an empathetic dialogue. In this chapter, through engaging with the work of bell hooks, I have exposed key aspects of Black feminist principles such as an ethic of care. As an arts-based tutor activist, this has assisted me to develop effective strategies to decolonise my practice in higher education.

This chapter explored class and race perspectives in arts-based feminist research and pedagogic practices by drawing upon the voices of the marginalised in conversations with the author. I drew upon the inspirational work of Black feminist bell hooks, in helping to navigate the challenges we face in the neoliberal university of the twenty-first century. As a feminist scholar, I have woven my experiences with hers and those with whom I share their stories. This is in the hope of decolonising the academy through acknowledging and resisting traditional race, class, and ableist epistemologies to explore identities in narratives of the marginalised.

Learning objective

Understand how visual arts-based approaches inspired by Black feminist thought, help demystify the decolonising programme in higher education.

As a practitioner, how might you apply the ethos of bell hooks's understanding of "care of the soul"?

Theme Three: Leading and delivering Black and decolonial feminist approaches in higher education

5
Resisting the neoliberal higher education academy

A decolonising feminist imaginary for existing in and surviving the neoliberal university

Kerry Harman

Introduction

This chapter explores how a "decolonising feminist imaginary" might be understood and how it might contribute to ongoing decolonisation work in the academy taking place in many parts of the world (Bhambra et al., 2018; Campt, 2017; Lugones, 2010; Mbembe, 2016; Rigney, 1999; Rivera Cusicanqui, 2012). I draw on my experiences as a feminist activist educator and researcher in the academy (in England) over the past ten years to think about neoliberalism (which refers to a political and economic approach that emphasises market-driven policies, competition, and efficiency, often at the expense of social welfare and equity. In higher education, it manifests as funding cuts, increased tuition fees, and a focus on marketable skills over critical thinking) and globalisation in higher education in the United Kingdom, ongoing knowledge hierarchies in English universities, and how these are currently being resisted.

The starting point for the chapter is that theory and practices are completely intertwined and that narrative and storying are important ways of producing feminist knowledges (Etienne, 2016). I will introduce and discuss some of the feminist theorists who have influenced my thinking on knowledge production processes and who provide resources for imagining a more equal and gender just world. As bell hooks (1989, p. 24) identified many years ago: "The separation of grassroots ways of sharing feminist thinking across kitchen tables from the spheres where much of that thinking is generated, the academy, undermines feminist movement". In other words, feminist activism and feminist theory building should not be separated. I propose a "decolonising feminist imaginary" that provides a useful way of both conceptualising and doing education in higher education as it enables attention to be directed to gendered, racialised, classist, heteronormative, and ableist practices in higher education in the United Kingdom but in ways that, hopefully, contribute to providing spaces for other ways of knowing, personal accountability, and being, for both students and staff.

I develop this line of thinking by describing curriculum changes that have been introduced on programmes that I have worked on collectively with colleagues at a University of London College, UK, and I discuss the processes for making those changes. Some of those colleagues have also provided chapters in this book. However, as Obasi (2019, p. 250) asks: "Has the hegemonic structure [within the academy] really changed" and does adding a "dash of colour" make a difference?". While decolonising the curriculum is key work and helps counter what Ahmed (2017, p. 152) refers to as "White men: a citational relation", I contend that those working within the academy must also consider the ways academic knowledges are produced (and reproduced) in order to provide more expansive and less parochial ways of knowing and understanding the world. We feminist activist scholars with an interest in decolonisation work need to continue developing ways to centre the knowledges of marginalised and oppressed groups.

The theoretical resources that I draw on have shifted over time and hopefully more directly acknowledge the vital contribution of Black feminist scholars, anticolonial theorists, and women of colour activists to theorising ontological politics. Ahmed (2017) reminds us that "things come to life when they are not overlooked" (p. 248). This chapter weaves in that thinking, the ways it underpins my teaching and research practices, and the tensions that continuing to practice in a neoliberal university in the United Kingdom creates when my colleagues are no longer employed on the programme they contributed to developing. I have survived in the academy but many of my colleagues have not, and this has not been a comfortable chapter to write. Nor should it be. The central question explored in this chapter is how might we activist feminists continue to work together collectively to open up spaces for thinking and existing during these violent neoliberal times? I have found Emejulu and Bassel's (2020) concept of the politics of exhaustion useful to think with in this exploration.

Who am I?

In writing this chapter, I have been asked: Who are you? What is your background?

To be honest, I have no idea who I "am". Here's a narrative to try and stitch together some of the fragments. I grew up and was educated to year 11 during the 1960s and 1970s in Newcastle, Australia. This was a working-class town, but my parents had middle-class aspirations. Dad was what some call "a self-made man". He left school at the age of 14 to work as a clerk at Muswellbrook Gas Company but returned to education as a mature student in his 40s and qualified as an accountant. My parents didn't have a lot of money, much less in fact than many of my friends whose fathers worked in the local mines. Mum was a reluctant homemaker. She'd been trained as an aeroplane engineer during World War II, but like many "good women" following the war dutifully got married and had four children. She loved her family, but I always had the sense she was never fully satisfied in the role of "mother". Both my parents were Protestants and active in their local church for as long as I can remember. I hated church and I hated the local state-funded school I attended and couldn't wait to leave. I married a working-class man at 18, we lived in a working-class suburb called Redhead, and we had a beautiful daughter when I was 20. Moving to Redhead was my immersion in working-class life. Many parts of it I loved. I loved the sense of community and helping each other out. Some parts I hated. I hated that everyone knew what everyone else was doing, and I hated that men ruled in that little township. Men did whatever they felt like, and women were meant to be loyal wives. They were "sluts" if they weren't. I went to art school between 1980 and 1983, and I then went on to practise as a feminist artist in the community for over ten years. While I was still married, I often went fishing with my husband and we sold the fish to make money. My husband, who was a ceramic tiler-fisherman, and I divorced in 1989. Approximately ten years later, he died of cardiac arrest from a drug overdose. He was on a waiting list to have a heart bypass at the time but was Hep-C positive, unemployed, had been in prison, and I expect was at the bottom of the waiting list. Telling our 17-year-old daughter that her father was dead was the most difficult thing I've ever had to do.

During the 1990s, I returned to education and put myself through undergraduate study, then postgraduate, then a doctoral degree at different universities and in different cities in Australia. I also worked in the community sector as an art teacher, initially, and then as a training and development coordinator of entry-level skills training programmes for those seeking (or for some, forced into seeking) employment. While I was completing my master's research degree in organisational studies (similar to an MPhil in the United Kingdom), I worked in my next-door neighbour's brothel as a receptionist. I washed the towels, answered the phone, booked appointments, and most importantly, handled the cash. My neighbour wanted a person she could trust to manage the money the nights she wasn't working at the parlour. I threw in the job the night her ex-boyfriend and member of the "Comanchero's" bike club threatened he was going to "close down" the parlour. I have been in a long-term relationship since the mid-1990s with a man who fled Czechoslovakia before the Velvet Revolution and sought political asylum in Australia. We migrated to the United Kingdom in 2006 when he took up a lecturer post in industrial design at the University of Northumbria. We have lived in the United Kingdom since then. I have never been assessed but I expect I am neurodiverse. My daughter is, and I have a strong hunch my mother was too. Various close family members have also been diagnosed. Many of my family (including me) also suffer from depression and require medication. I am a White cis woman with predominantly Scottish and English heritage, but I also had a dual heritage grandfather from Sri Lanka. I am a grandmother of a dual heritage grandson. I started my first permanent academic appointment in 2012 at the age of 52. So, tell me, who am I? Perhaps one unifying thread that weaves through my fragmented life is: I am a feminist.

A decolonising feminist imaginary

My call in this chapter for a decolonising feminist imaginary follows from the extensive contribution to feminist thinking by Black feminist, Afro-feminist, Latinx, and Indigenous scholars (e.g. Collins, 2000; hooks, 1989, 2000; Lugones, 2003; Moraga and Anzaldúa, 1983; Moreton-Robinson, 2000; Oyewumi, 2002). As all these feminist theorists are only too aware, the Western philosophical tradition has contributed to the ongoing exclusion of knowledges and other ways of knowing from marginalised groups. This means that particular groups and particular things remain unheard, unattended to, invisible, and thus fail to exist. In other words, what does and what (seemingly) does not "exist" is political. The politics of existing (and survival) is evoked by Emejulu and Sobande in their book titled *To Exist Is to Resist* (2019). This powerful collection of essays by European Black feminist scholars enacts ontological politics as they write themselves into existence in the text.

The importance of survival and "finding ways to exist in a world that makes it difficult to exist" is also foregrounded by Sara Ahmed in *Living a Feminist Life* (2017, p. 239). She is also acutely aware of ontological politics and, again, this is also linked with her experiences of exclusion as a woman of colour. She turns to Black feminist scholars to provide further insight, as who knows better about survival than a Black feminist woman? Surviving has been the everyday experience for so many Black feminists, both inside and outside the university. As Lorde (1980) so powerfully contends: "Caring for myself is not self-indulgence, it is self-preservation, and that is an act of political warfare" (1988, p. 131). This oft-repeated statement needs to keep being repeated, to keep being cited, over and over, again and again. But it must never be separated from who wrote it. It was written by a Black feminist and speaks directly about her experience of ontological politics. Ahmed contends that rather than understanding this text as an expression of self-preservation, in an individualised sense, it represents a collective resistance to racialised oppression. In caring about herself and continuing to exist, Lorde is at the same time NOT attending to the needs of those she "should" be caring about but refuses to, that is, those with White privilege.

This overt resistance to White privilege works to amplify the political potency of the statement.

Ahmed also draws on the inspirational work of bell hooks and Patricia Hill Collins (among many other Black feminist scholars) in *Living a Feminist Life*. Both these scholars have used feminist praxis as a way of discussing and producing other ways of knowing. For example, hooks (1989) reminds us that:

> It would further feminist movement if new feminist thinking could be once again shared in small group contexts, integrating critical analysis with discussion of personal experience. It would be useful to promote anew the small group setting as an arena for education for critical consciousness, so that women and men might come together in neighborhoods and communities to discuss feminist concerns. (p. 24)

While these words are over 30 years old, they still resonate and they have been influential in the way I conduct research, particularly current research on sensory ways of knowing care. The research team on the Reimagining Homecare project, which is a strand of a larger Arts and Humanities Research Council Aesthetics (AHRCA) Arts and Humanities Research Council Aesthetics (AHRCA)-funded Care Aesthetics Research project, have worked collaboratively to produce collective feminist knowledges about caregiving and what it feels like to be a caregiver (Firmin and Harman, 2024). Importantly, the project has provided the space to experiment with research forms that hopefully enable more expansive and less parochial knowledges to be produced about caregiving. In breaking with traditional forms of knowledge production with academics typically in the role of knowledge producer, and caregivers and caregiving as their object of knowledge, our experimental forms of collective knowledge production have created new research possibilities and new caring infrastructures within the academy (Harman et al., forthcoming).

Moreover, Collins, in her classic text titled *Black Feminist Thought: Knowledge, Consciousness, and the Politics of Empowerment*, which was first published in 1990, stresses that "Afrocentric" ways of knowing are understood as dangerous as they "call into question the content of what currently passes as truth and simultaneously challenge the processes of arriving at the truth" (p. 271). She argues that processes of "connection" and "caring" underpin African epistemologies rather than distance and separation. The ongoing attempt to separate the subject and object, which has prevailed in Western philosophy, is thus challenged by these other ways of knowing. Both these scholars have made significant contributions in terms of how we (academics) might do pedagogy and how we might do research. They each emphasise the importance of centring marginalised knowledges in the academy and the politics associated with this type of work.

Furthermore, in "Toward a Decolonial Feminism", Lugones (2010) asserts that an understanding of a gendered world using a male-female dichotomy (as well as all the other dichotomies of modernism) is a colonial construction. She argues that many non-modern societies did not think and organise that way, and the separation of "male" and "female" is not as unambiguous as Western ways of knowing and categorising have suggested.

Indeed, Lugones (along with other scholars) contends that the "coloniality of gender" was the outcome of forcing people into racialised gendered categories. This leads her to advocating more nuanced readings of resistances to power through a "fractured locus" that comes from outside the logic of capitalism. Her work points to the importance of collectives and communities, which she argues are the starting point for an intersubjective understanding of self: "Subject, relations, ground, and possibilities are continually transformed, incarnating a weave from the fractured locus that constitutes a creative, peopled re-creation" (p. 754). All these feminist scholars point to disrupting dominant Western binaries and how we might make knowledges in ways that challenge the dichotomies which have prevailed in the Western academy. This includes attending to "what matters" and getting close to, rather than distancing ourselves from, our objects of study. This is collective work, and as Ahmed (2017, p. 236) reminds us, "Feminism needs feminists to survive". However, before further discussing what a decolonising feminist imaginary might offer as a tactic for survival, I provide the broader context for why this is so urgently needed in English universities.

The rise and rise of neoliberalism in English higher education

The broader context for the personal narrative provided in this chapter is the ongoing dominance of neoliberal ideology as it is operationalised in organisational practices and policy in English higher education. This fact has been well documented by numerous scholars (Maisuria and Cole, 2017; Radice, 2015; Rustin, 2016), and I will not repeat their cogent analyses here. It is taken as a given in this chapter, then, that we (English, higher education academics) exist within a neoliberal policy context, both at the broader level of government policy and at the more local level of policies at our institutions where we work. A fundamental principle in a neoliberal landscape is that universities should be in competition with each other and that the market will decide which universities get to "exist" (Metcalf, 2017).

Indeed, a neoliberal ideology not only affects universities and academics in England and the United Kingdom, but it could also be described as a global phenomenon (Gibbons, 2018). For example, Harney and Moten (2013), among others, provide a powerful critique of universities and the ways they are integrally intertwined with capitalism. In *The Undercommons: Fugitive Planning & Black Study*, they point to the ongoing exploitation of students through accruing debt through fees, and the exploitation of teaching staff, particularly those on sessional (or casual) contracts. They poetically attend to the separations and hierarchies perpetuated in and through universities, including the separation of teaching and research:

> But it is teaching that brings us in. Before there are grants, research, conferences, books, and journals there is the experience of being taught and of teaching. Before the research post with no teaching, before the graduate students to mark the exams, before the string of sabbaticals, before the permanent reduction in teaching load, the appointment to run the Center, the consignment of pedagogy to a discipline called education, before the course designed to be a new book, teaching happened.

> The moment of teaching for food is therefore often mistakenly taken to be a stage, as if eventually one should not teach for food. If the stage persists, there is a social pathology in the university. But if the teaching is successfully passed on, the stage is surpassed, and teaching is consigned to those who are known to remain in the stage, the sociopathological labor of the university (2013, p. 27).

The above passage is an acerbic reminder of the violence of the hierarchies perpetuated in and through universities with tenured "real academics" (the people who engage in research) offloading the labour of teaching to the casual teaching workforce, who are understood as inherently inferior and "sociopathic" because they perform the labour that is actually the core of the university. And nowhere is this violent separation more stark than in the university where I currently work. The Teaching and Scholarship staff are the supply of casual labour that enable UK universities to morph and adapt to the vicissitudes of neoliberalism. They are picked up and dropped off as enrolments on programmes increase or decrease/when research leave for permanent academics needs to be covered. This is "normal" in higher education institutions.

Surviving in a neoliberal university in England (or fewer people = more work = violence)

This particular narrative of the violences associated with continuing to *exist* in English higher education in neoliberal times commences with a programme that no longer exists at the College – the Higher Education Introductory Studies programme

(HEIS). This was an entry-level programme for mature learners who did not hold what are referred to as "traditional academic qualifications", and I was the programme director of HEIS. Various independent studies and reports showed the success of HEIS in providing access to, ongoing participation in, and successful completion of degree programmes in English higher education (Butcher et al., 2017; Callender et al., 2014). However, despite its remarkable success, the harsh economic environment in which UK universities continue to operate contributed to that programme's being replaced with a Foundation Year (FY) of study at the College. The FY provides the College with an additional year of full-time fees from students and a guaranteed flow of students to degree programmes in extremely competitive times, and this was very attractive to an organisation experiencing financial difficulty. When the FY was introduced in 2018, HEIS was phased out and many of the casual teaching and scholarship staff working on the programme were offered voluntary severance (VS). Most took this.

Unlike HEIS, the explicit ambition of the FY, as expressed by the senior executive of the College in various internal College communications, was income generation and "financial recovery". However, the outward-facing narrative presented by the College when speaking about the FY has always been couched in a discourse of widening participation. In other words, "widening participation" provided the "human face" externally for the College, for implementing a financial strategy for survival. Sadly, however, the very students enrolling on the FY degrees are often those that have been most let down by the compulsory education system in England. This is a system that continues to reproduce ongoing inequalities (Reay, 2012; Reay, 2018) and the students arriving to the FY at the College often carry with them the violences and failures experienced during their time in the compulsory education system. This group of students often need a wide range of very resource-intensive support in order to adapt to and successfully complete their programmes at university, and this was the type of support that had been provided in the HEIS programme. However, in a climate of ongoing fiscal constraint at the College, the resourcing of support for these students has largely fallen on the already very overstretched members of academic staff with permanent contracts in their roles as Personal Tutors (PTs) and leads as programme directors.

The care and attention that was given to students on HEIS is largely absent from the FY. This is exemplified in the blunt appraisal from a casual tutor teaching on one of the FY modules who had also worked previously on the HEIS programme. According to this Teaching and Scholarship (T&S) staff member: "no-one loves the foundation year" and, sadly, I'd have to agree. These students, many of whom fit the category of Black, Asian and Minority Ethnic (BAME) are largely neglected (yet again) and left to navigate their way through a largely inhospitable higher education system. Inevitably, some don't make it and are left with no qualification and a very large student debt (Adams, 2023; Callender and Mason, 2017).

Despite the ambition for financial recovery of the College, with the FY at the centre of its strategy, the harshness of the current neoliberal climate has led to its ongoing financial decline (Weale, 2022; Williams, 2023). As a response, further rounds of VS have been made during the past few years by the senior executive to encourage staff to leave as enrolments on programmes have declined. As part of that attrition, a VS was taken by the previous director of the MSc Education, Power and Social Change (EPSC) programme in 2019. The initial plan of the senior executive for that programme was for Teaching and Scholarship (T&S) staff working on the modules to teach out the MSc EPSC when this colleague left and then close the programme down.

The closure of HEIS, discussed earlier, resulted in the MSc EPSC remaining in the Department of Psychosocial Studies' portfolio. I was transferred to lead the programme in 2020. Since then, ongoing cost-cutting measures by senior executives have led to the loss of T&S staff who previously taught on the MSc, leaving the programme in a diminished and less diverse state. Despite this, senior management has shown no personal accountability. As the sole permanent staff member leading EPSC programmes, I face an ever-increasing workload and severe time constraints. Ironically, I also serve as the School lead for the FY programme. These challenges were compounded by a College restructure in the summer of 2023, further straining resources and staff capacity.

Following what some refer to as a process of "managed decline", further rounds of voluntary severances have been made to academic and professional services staff across the College. One department has now been merged with three other former departments, to form a new School of Social Sciences. This type of restructure, with the aim of cutting costs, is a typical executive management response in neoliberal times. The ongoing shrinking of the College is symptomatic of the anorexic university, and exhaustion, for those who remain at the College, is our everyday. Less people = more work. Questions around the demographics of those who remain and whether there were inequalities arising from the restructure have been asked but remain unanswered.

In summary, the prevailing neoliberal ideology in English higher education has contributed to ongoing violences at the university where I work: to my colleagues, to me, and ultimately to students who enrol on programmes at the College. The question then is no longer "what is happening in higher education in the UK and why?" The impact of neoliberal ideology on universities in England is very clear. We live that daily. Rather, the question for academics concerned with the ongoing reproduction of raced, classist, ableist, gendered, and heteronormative inequalities and exclusions in higher education is: how might we work within the ruins of the English university and find ways of operating that not only sustain us and enable us to exist, but also keep disrupting "the long middle" of neoliberalism (Berlant, 2022, p. 77)?

Black feminist responses to neoliberal challenges

It is here that Emejulu and Bassel's concept of "the politics of exhaustion" (2020) is particularly useful. These scholars contend that in mutually recognising a shared exhaustion as a collective property, not just owned by individuals, spaces are opened up for a more mutual "conviviality". They propose that: "It can be possible to express the desire to build solidarity on terms that resist white supremacy, patriarchy and capitalism rather than conform to parameters set by the white left" (p. 405). Following Emejulu and Bassel, I am convinced that the formation of feminist collectives that read and enact the world though a decolonial logic are crucial to surviving in the neoliberal university. Their work suggests that the shared exhaustion arising from ongoing neoliberal violences in higher education might be a way of sustaining community and a mode of resistance. Crucially, they argue for specific spaces for women of colour as these women activists need political spaces where they no longer need to "assert their legitimacy" to "allies", which is itself exhausting work (p. 405). Indeed, the Womanism, Activism, Higher Education Research Network might be understood as a concrete example of the type of collective and convivial space for Black feminists and women of colour that are currently being created in higher education. This is a group of scholars who meet, hold conferences and seminars, publish, and develop ongoing strategy for surviving in the academy. The network provides an example of what Berlant (2022) refers to as heterotopian infrastructures "that sustain the mutations that emerge in popular resistance to austerity regimes and antiblack and patriarchal capitalism" (p. 115). The network provides a space for solidarity in English higher education and less parochial ways of knowing.

The collaborative writing practices of Emejulu and Bassel also point to productive relationships between Black feminist scholars and allies working to decolonise the academy, and it is this terrain that the Womanism, Activism, Higher Education Research Network also navigates. While the network organises spaces and events specifically for Black feminists and women of colour, they also work collectively with academics who are interested in decolonising the academy and disrupting structural inequalities reproduced by higher education institutions. The collection of essays in this book is one example of the network's collaborations with allies. However, it is critical to stress that the starting point for any collective work is what Bassel (2017) refers to as a "politics of listening". This is about ensuring that practices are developed for listening to and centring the voices of groups that have been previously marginalised. Using the convivial atmospheres created in and through a "politics of exhaustion" as a frame, recent and current experiments in opening up normative enclosures within the academy are discussed in the section that follows.

Decolonising feminist collectives and surviving the neoliberal university

The Decolonising the Academy Collective, which was established in 2020, provides another example of a collective space for furthering decolonising work inspired by a feminist imaginary. The Collective formed as a response to growing calls by students for the inclusion of theory from scholars from the Global South *as well as* the inclusion of anti-racist pedagogies in their courses (Bhambra et al., 2018). The topic of "decolonising the academy" was linked to the teaching and research interests of the core members of the collective who were using critical race theory/Black feminist scholarship/feminist research approaches and more expansive ways for producing knowledges within the academy. The notion of praxis and making knowledges in and through collective struggle was intertwined with the thinking and approaches of all the group members. The point of mobilisation for the Collective was the Womanist Ways of Learning conference in 2018, led by one of the group's core members.

Following that conference, the core working group embarked on a series of meetings with academics from other universities who were also working on decolonising their institutions, and we ran an event to launch the Decolonising the Curriculum work at in 2019. Professors Gurminder Bhambra and Meera Sabaratnam both spoke at the event. Their powerful accounts, as well as those from a student and the chair of the working group, inspired the team members to continue this work even though there was initially no support from the institution. That changed in 2021, and after obtaining a small seed grant to establish the Decolonising the Academy Collective, we organised a series of seminars and invited scholars working in the area of decolonisation to speak on topics related to teaching, research, student experience, and institutional change. These events were very well attended, with over 500 people attending the inaugural online event in 2011 where Kehinde Andrews spoke on the topic of "Decolonising the Academy: Education, Power and Social Change".

The Decolonising the Academy meetings provided a rich and sustaining space for dialogue and discussing decolonising practices and approaches. Since the initial conference in 2018, my colleagues in the Decolonising the Academy group have been extremely generous mentors in the area of decolonisation, and our discussions have underpinned the ongoing development of the MSc in EPSC at Birkbeck. A "decolonising feminist imaginary" now provides the overarching framework for the programme, and this includes the introduction of Black feminist literature and literature from feminist Indigenous scholars and feminist scholars from the Global South to frame how we might think about knowledge production in the academy and whose knowledges get to count. The notion of feminist praxis is an important concept in the programme. EPSC students are encouraged to use feminist praxis as a way of developing their pedagogic knowledges and practices throughout the programme.

Another feminist collective space is the Feminist Imaginary Research Network (FIRN). This international collaboration between feminist adult education scholars, feminist artist activists, and members of the International Association of Women's Museums (IAWM; iawm.international) is working on a number of funded projects exploring the "feminist imaginary" and its contribution to social change and transformation. A shared interest underpinning the work of FIRN is how arts-based pedagogies and research approaches can be used as tools for disrupting White supremacist, capitalist patriarchy (Clover et al., 2022; Dickson and Clover, 2021). The FIRN collective organises workshops, events, exhibitions, and publications to share practices and engage in arts-based research. A current collaboration is the organisation of the *Visible-Invisible* exhibition, and work that is contributed will be exhibited at various sites across the globe. A principle underpinning these feminist imaginary exhibitions is the idea of "living knowledge" and an expansive approach to producing knowledge on various feminist themes. Not only do the people responding to the Call have the opportunity for contributing their experiences and responses but those visiting the exhibition also have the opportunity to contribute.

The multidisciplinary, multi-institutional, and global interconnections of the FIRN collective enable a rich and vital space for exchange and sustenance. FIRN members are from the Global

South and the Global North, and this is a critical element in the organisation of the group. The IAWM members have an incredibly rich experience in curating women's exhibitions that disrupt White supremacist, capitalist patriarchy; the feminist artist activist members have been disrupting White supremacist, capitalist patriarchy in various ways with their artwork/performances; and the feminist adult educators share their research practices, including strategies for engaging with marginalised groups, in an effort to create gender justice and broader social change (Clover et al., 2014; Clover et al., 2022).

A decolonising feminist imaginary also underpins the work and focus of the Reconceptualising Resilience: Home, Community Care and Ubuntu project in South Africa. I was provided with an extraordinary learning opportunity when I was asked to join this feminist collective. The work is being led by Professor Gubela Mji, who has been researching in the area of Indigenous women's knowledges in healthcare for over a decade (Ohajunwa and Mji, 2021). The project aims to strengthen healthcare services in the informal healthcare sector in South Africa through developing a better understanding of how health and well-being are understood and practised by women carers in marginalised communities. At present, these ways of knowing and caring, which are often underpinned by an African philosophy of Ubuntu, are overlooked in the development of healthcare policy which has been dominated by Western models of health. However, the health practitioners working on the project believe more sustainable health practices can be developed through incorporating Indigenous knowledges. This is another experiment in "reimagining care".

A reflexive engagement with "the politics of exhaustion"

I could not survive in the academy without the decolonial feminist collectives that continue to sustain, nurture, and renew me. They enable me to make sense of what I am doing and to prioritise what I need to keep working on. But how to avoid having survival and continuing to exist becoming individual acts of self-preservation and thus reinforcing a neoliberal "survival of the fittest" mentality and the violences this produces? Some may have already felt a twinge of discomfort or even a searing pain as I call on Black feminist literature to discuss my ongoing White existence in the academy. And what about those who are no longer working on the EPSC programme and the violences they have encountered? One of the T&S staff who developed the programme many years ago and had contributed to its ongoing development for over a decade has left. Another colleague who had developed the Education, Globalisation and Change module and was convening that module using a Black feminist framework is no longer employed. Is it just "too bad" that these academics no longer teach on the programme? Is it mere coincidence that the one survivor is a cis White woman? The T&S teaching team all came from marginalised social groups, and this points to the gendered, classist, racialised, and ableist inequalities associated with casualisation in English higher education. Moreover, it also points to the links with the broader market forces that executive management teams in English universities have adopted wholesale with little struggle and little thinking through.

While many academics, including me, have been involved in organising collectively and participating in industrial action over a number of years to try and improve the working conditions for all academics in the United Kingdom, especially for those working on casual contracts, is the collective work I do as an active member of a trade union, including striking, enough from a decolonising feminist imaginary approach? Is there a time when White feminist academics need to rethink their survival in the academy? Is holding open the fragile space of a fragile programme by continuing to exist sufficient? Some might argue the educational goals of the programme and the work that it does justify keeping it going. However, should a course underpinned by the concept of ontological politics be taught by a White feminist academic? It doesn't seem "right".

Returning to the central question, then, how do we academics in English universities continue working together collectively to open up spaces for thinking and being that are underpinned by a decolonising feminist imaginary? And linked with that, is it possible to do that in the neoliberal university? The collection of essays in this book is an example of one way of centring and continuing decolonising feminist conversations. Collective writing spaces continue to be a key element in enacting a decolonising feminist imaginary. A collective and diverse teaching team contributes to the vitality of the programme, and the violences of neoliberalism desperately need correcting and nowhere is this more urgent than in the neoliberal university. And until that happens, perhaps those who remain need to just "keep […] showing up" (Berlant, 2022, p. 172). Or is it time to rethink our strategies, to "bail out", and to join the collective undercommons?

In the next chapter, we shift from examining the perspective of White working-class feminism to exploring what it means to be a Black feminist and activist. We delve into the significance of conducting Black feminist research with the ultimate goal of decolonising the academy.

Learning objective

Understand how senior management in higher education might be encouraged to include decolonial and Black feminist approaches in their day-to-day work to help improve equality, diversity, and inclusion outcomes.

6
Combahee and beyond

Black feminism, activism, and decolonising approaches to research

Nandita Sirker

> "If Black women were free; it would mean that every-
> one else would have to be free since our freedom
> would necessitate the destruction of all the systems
> of oppression."

These words were written by the Combahee River Collective in 1977 (Combahee River Collective, 2015). I argue that these words are as relevant today as when they were first written.

Introduction

This chapter provides an exploration of the relationship between Black feminist/womanist theory, scholarship, and action for liberation and social justice, and what it means to be a Black feminist academic and teacher. The chapter deploys Black feminist theory to examine how we as Black women can survive and thrive in the academy and what can be done by us and others to support and nurture students who are marginalised by Whiteness, misogyny, and heteronormativity. Like other contributors to this volume, I am deeply concerned about the urgent need to decolonise the academy, making it a safer, more affirming place for students and academics who are currently "othered" within it. I want to work with others to make the academy a place where we are seen as not just subjects of research or "community representatives" but as creators of knowledge whose lived experience and scholarship can inform teaching and scholarship widely, not just within the narrow and increasingly marginalised and resource-poor areas of race and gender studies. As Moffat-Batteau (2015) observes, "these disciplinary boundaries unfortunately have the result of rendering the study and practice of feminist intellectual work invisible to the rest of the academy" (p. 54).

As highlighted by my fellow contributors, there is an urgent need to share strategies to resist and survive within what is for many of us a hostile environment where we are at best tolerated but often undermined and ignored.

In this work I argue that Black feminist theory with its focus on Intersectional analysis (Crenshaw, 1989) and its validation of lived experience has, over the last 50 years continued to provide a body of scholarship and an analytical framework which is still very relevant today. I show how a new generation of Black British women and their allies use Black feminist theory to analyse and organise around contemporary issues such as, transphobia, and state violence against Black women and Black men both in the diaspora and via the domination of European and American political and economic interests across the globe.

Producing theory from lived experience – Finding our voice

I came to Black feminism in the 1970s and 1980s – the child of an Asian immigrant father and a White working-class mother. We experienced racist microaggressions and direct acts of hostility and violence daily. That time was the era of Suspected Person Law (SUS), the rise of the National Front, when 13 young Black people died in a fire which was started by racists in New Cross. Prior to that, Altab Ali and other Asian men were killed by gangs of youths, and the police looked more interested in criminalising Black youths to curb what the popular press called a "mugging epidemic" (Hall, 2019) than in protecting people from acts of racial violence. To be a Black or Asian woman was to be ignored, stereotyped, subject to both state and male violence. In activist work and other struggles, we were often forced to choose between the misogyny which was rife in anti-racist Black organisations, and the erasure and our misnaming as Black women in mainstream feminism.

I have been an activist, a journalist, a mother, and a professional working with children and families for over 40 years. For me, like Lewis (2020) and other Black sisters whose work I have read, Black feminism has been the framework in which I have lived, loved, and struggled. It has held me in its "warm embrace" (Mirza 2015), and has shaped me as a mother, daughter, lover, comrade, and the social justice-minded student I now try to be. Black feminism is an appeal to wholeness, to being our real authentic, unedited selves allowing us to see and celebrate the complexity of our lives and identities. Black feminism is life -and joyous. It gave me and many others the courage to define ourselves in our own terms. However, at times involvement in it was a difficult and painful process. There were rifts between different groups of women within the movement, differences in ethnicity, differences between straight women and lesbians. Issues such as domestic violence and abortion also caused divisions, and many of the organisations and alliances formed split as a result. It was a troubled and sad time, but some of us emerged from this more convinced than ever that only Black feminist theory provided us with the tools to listen. We were determined to reflect deeply and form alliances across our differences with White women and progressive men and to be active within our communities on our own terms.

As a young woman, I read the inspiring works of Black feminist writers theorising from their lived experience and making connections across the diaspora and back "home". Black feminists linked race, gender, and class in meaningful, rigorous explorations, showing how these themes structured our lives. The work of Black women like Audre Lorde (1980) and June Jordan (2002), along with anthologies containing the writings of authors such as Grewal (1992), Kay (1988), Parmar (1984), Landor (1988), and Lewis (1988), as well as other important works such as the essay "Charting the Journey and Challenging Imperial Feminism" (Amos and Parmar, 1984), helped me and many others to find our space and our voice in both feminist and anti-racist struggles. These works enabled us to organize around the issues that concerned us in ways we felt comfortable and safe. Later in my professional life and academic career, I became inspired by and motivated by the work of sisters like Gail Lewis (2000) and Suriya Nayak (2019) who use Black feminist analysis to examine how and why social work and associated professions are not meeting the needs of Black women and their families, and how Black feminist theory can be mobilised to create emancipatory practice. The productive and celebratory potential of difference as expressed by Lorde (2015) and the insistence on both lived experience in all its complexity embodied in the work of Patricia Hill Collins (2000, 2019) have provided me with the tools I need to think, write, and reflect on how I work as a teacher professionally and what I produce as an academic.

Black feminism in the academy – teaching with love – a decolonising tool

In 2020, Gail Lewis wrote that "Black British Feminism is a move to inject raced/gendered reflexivity into academia" (2020, p. 6) for those of us who teach using these principles. This means thinking carefully on how we do this and how we embody our key principles – doing what bell hooks (2003) calls "teaching with love". This has determined my scholarship and practice as it demands that we reflect constantly and deeply on how our work in the academy links with other facets of our lives. While it is true that our very presence in the academy is an act of resistance, a refusal to accept the place allocated to people like us in what El-Enany (2020) so eloquently described as a space of "coloniality" (referring to the United Kingdom), I argue, we need to do more than this if we are to really teach with love and move forward in decolonising the academy. hooks (2020) reminds us that as Black women we occupy a unique space from which we can create theory and practice which is emancipatory because "we have not to be socialised to assume the role of exploiter or oppressor in that we are allowed no 'institutionalised other' that we can exploit or oppress" (p. 16).

This is a position of enormous potential, one which, as hooks reminds us, can be used to challenge, and create "a counter hegemony" (p. 16), but also it is not without risk as those of us who attempt to teach, write, and theorise from this perspective are often attacked and marginalised even by White feminist colleagues. "Attempts by white feminists to silence Black women are rarely written about. All too often they take place in conference rooms, classrooms or in the privacy of cosy living rooms" (hooks, 2020, p. 13).

I returned to education five years ago, more than 30 years since being an undergraduate – back then I was "a fish out of water" – a Brown girl from West London, educated in an all-girls comprehensive where university was very firmly NOT on the agenda. It was only my father's relentless determination to ensure I would "succeed", his constant reminders that I had to be twice as good as everyone else because of my race and gender, and his refusal to allow me to have any degree of independence while I lived under his roof which saved me from a life as a typist, hairdresser, or nursery nurse – all professions to which I was and am completely unsuited. My teachers were all dedicated to guiding us all into these occupations – or similar ones – and were adamant that university was not (in the words of my careers teacher) "for girls like you dear".

I therefore arrived at university with high hopes – I had been brought up to believe that racism was the result of ignorance and that education and educated people would therefore be different, better, more enlightened. I quickly learned that what "education", or more accurately class privilege, did was to allow racism to be expressed in more subtle and less obvious ways. Instead of being called "Paki" at bus stops, I was told "how well" I had done and asked with great concern whether my parents had opposed my coming to university because they wanted me to have an arranged marriage. After a few difficult weeks, I found others like me – Asian, Caribbean, African students, all of us looking for a "home" in a hostile space, and others who had an interest in decolonising, anti-racist, and feminist politics. We read, we talked, we argued, and we struggled, and through this I discovered radical Black writers, theorists, and activists and, most importantly, Black feminism.

When I returned to education to begin my master's study as an adult, I chose a subject and programme which I hoped would embrace and embody this. What I found were dedicated teachers who genuinely engaged with us "with love" who supported and encouraged me to pursue my dream of completing a PhD. However, I also found that the scholarship on which they based their teaching and therefore what we needed to engage with and understand was overwhelmingly drawn from the work produced by White feminists and critical theorists – people like them. There appeared to be no framework for seriously decolonising the academy. I found it hard to understand why we studied Foucault (1970, 1978), not Fanon (1952) and/or Butler (1990), not Spillers (1987) or Wynters (2002). Black feminism, race, and empire were consigned to the margins – and with them those of us whose life experiences drew us to them. They were not invisible exactly, but were the terrain of a few brave and dedicated Black academics around us, whom we gathered and who provided us with inspiration and encouragement.

Now as both a student with two hugely supportive Black supervisors and as a teacher, teaching masters and undergraduate students, I am regularly reminded that we still exist on the margins despite our relative privilege – as academics, and as diasporic subjects who enjoy the security of citizenship. In recognition of this and guided by the theory produced by Black women, I am conscious also of the responsibility I have towards my students – to exercise the "ethic of care" which is a key tenet of Black feminist theory and from which I have benefited and continue to benefit from.

As a Black feminist I must always recognise the connection between what we teach and write and the wider struggles in our lives, and the lives and struggles of people of colour in the diaspora and beyond. Black feminist theory is internationalist and unites us as sisters in struggle across the globe – both in similarity and in celebration of our differences. It provides those of us who are the products of an education system which privileges White, Christian scholarship over other forms of knowledge, with an alternative in which people outside Europe and settler colonialist states are producers of knowledge, creators of great works of art and literature. Reading the work of scholars from Africa, Asia, from Latin America and the Caribbean, reminds those of us who have lived our lives constantly under the White gaze, always seen as other, as less than, and as belonging to inferior backward cultures that we are more than that. Scholarship from these places is from a different perspective – critical of imperialism and its devastating effects certainly, but from a position of confidence and belonging which is often hard to find in the diaspora. It reminds us that while the struggles we face may stem from the same root, the form in which they appear are different – sisterhood may be universal, but women's experiences are very different, mediated by class, race, and location, and we in the West, as Spivak so powerfully wrote, do not speak for the "subaltern" – for all our sisters. They have their own voice and we must listen to that.

There is much we can learn from our sisters in academia across the diaspora as the fight to decolonise the academy is one which is being fought across America, the Pacific, and Europe. We see from Tanya Buckhard's experience teaching in the United States that, despite the body of scholarship and activism from those who came before us and the profound effect sisters like hooks, Lorde, Collins, and Crenshaw have had on feminist theory, racism, victimisation, and hate speech are still alive and well in US campuses just as they are here in the United Kingdom and Europe.

We are still on the margins, and the attacks on critical race theory both here and in the United States would suggest that in fact we are losing ground, not gaining it. Nevertheless, the fact that we are now able to read, reference, and recommend to students a growing canon of work outlining Black feminist methodological approaches, and the more widespread recognition of the value of these approaches and of the pioneering work of scholars like Linda Tawhai Smith to the production of critical theoretical work – across social sciences – is a cause for cautious joy and optimism.

With this also comes great responsibility, a commitment to deep reflection and to being challenged as well as to being challenging, to create theory and practice pedagogy which moves beyond simplistic binaries and essentialist identity politics and which links to wider struggles for social justice. Black feminism is the intellectual and spiritual home of intersectionality – a commitment to understanding how oppressions of class, of race, of gender and heteronormativity act in articulation with one another. It is this commitment that lies behind the Combahee declaration (1977). A commitment to this in both activism and practice requires us to think and reflect on difference and to listen carefully to those voices that speak of experiences which are different to or unfamiliar to our own. Theorists such as Crenshaw, Collins, Mohanty, and Evans-Winters illustrate how Black feminists/womanists embrace the challenge of producing theory using what Mirza (2015) describes as "embodied intersectionality" (p. 4), which can accurately reflect the complex reality of lives that are lived within intersecting domains of power.

Our voices are often heard faintly – if at all. Lewis (2005) identifies the presence of Black women in the academy as a form of resistance to erasure "fleshy, experiential and epistemological" (p. 14).

Our work is present, decolonising, but often ignored by mainstream academia or confined to narrow disciplinary boundaries. Within mainstream social sciences and feminist studies, Black feminist theory and scholarship are not recognised as having any useful application to wider fields of study (Moffat Bateau, 2015).

My responsibility, therefore, as a teacher and researcher are to resist this by ensuring that I centre both my scholarship and my teaching on the work of Black feminist and other Black scholars whose work is too often marginalised. I see it as our responsibility as Black feminists to reject the increasingly cut-throat neoliberal ideology which pervades educational institutions by actively rejecting competition with each other – choosing instead to support and celebrate each other's work. Teaching with love means we need to be respectful of students, of the life experience they bring, and invite them to question existing paradigms, while creating an atmosphere where it is safe to explore and question.

Above all, those of us who have a place, however tenuous, within the academy must prepare a place and ease the path of those who come after us. In a decolonising agenda we must model the change we wish to see, although the pressure of zero-hour contracts and funding constraints makes that daily task more difficult. We must continue to argue for the adoption of our key tenets – of intersectionality, of an unwillingness to leave anyone behind, and of the use of first-person narratives which privilege lived experience across all academic disciplines, and that our marginality is a strength which has produced theory that listens to and respects the voice of marginalised people.

Motherhood and "refugeeness" – Can you see us?

Black feminist theory and a conscious commitment to intersectionality demand that we link our scholarship to political and social issues which are relevant to our struggles within the diaspora and with people in Africa, Asia, the Caribbean, and Latin America in the knowledge that imperialism has not disappeared. There is no postcolonial, just a new colonial formation which continues to require the subjugation – both materially and intellectually – of Black and Brown bodies (El-Enany, 2020). Research is never neutral – even if Whiteness serves to obscure this and to present racial and gender-based injustice as an aberration as opposed to a conscious pattern of ordering and Western social cultural and religious norms as universal. Therefore, our job as Black feminist academics is to produce research which "talks back and disrupts these narratives and makes visible those who have been erased. Scholarship which is truly intersectional is never just for its own sake – it must be linked to the pursuit of social justice claims" (Collins, 2019).

My chosen research area – refugee mothers in the UK – emerged from my lived experience and professional life working with families affected by homelessness, and HIV and AIDs. Later, I worked within early years, Sure Start local programmes, prevention, and early intervention services. I found that refugee families were either problematised as "hard to reach" and as having trouble "adjusting", or were ignored completely as increasingly hostile discourse and public policy focused professionals' attention on whether they were eligible, under no recourse and asylum rules to access services.

Any attempts by professionals to work collaboratively and inclusively with refugee communities were viewed as complicated at best and often simply undesirable. I was told quite firmly that my efforts to include refugee families in Sure Start services were "not a priority" with local politicians as they were not part of what the politicians perceived as the "local community", and the concern was that other neighbouring areas were not prioritising this and therefore we would be "swamped" by refugee families from other areas. I was advised by senior managers to focus on "established" local communities – a view that was shared by some partner agencies and colleagues who saw any work done with refugee families as taking away resources from local White working-class and Caribbean families. Interestingly, these same people did not view the high numbers of relatively affluent White families who had recently moved into our rapidly gentrifying corner of West London in the same light – they were welcomed, as one of them told me without a trace of irony, and told that "Sure Start is for everyone". More than 15 years later as I returned to study, the clamour to "protect our borders, to stop the boats and to preserve the British way of life" has become deafening.

Refugees and asylum seekers are criminalised and deliberately excluded from accessing basic services – health and social care, and housing are now all the new "borders" policed unwillingly by public sector workers who entered these professions never anticipating this would become a day-to-day part of their job description. We are subjected to images of men, women, and children drowned and washed up in European holiday resorts and sea-side towns, but their stories and struggles are rarely told; instead, we are fed ever more alarmist statistics about the threat posed by forced migration from war and persecution. Increasingly, this reality is elided by the renaming of refugees as "illegal migrants" drawn to the rich pickings to be had from our benefits system.

The Black body, the racialised other of colonial discourse, has found its modern resting place in the figure of the refugee – to be reviled and repelled, not welcomed, as their suffering and the physical and emotional pain experienced by them is less than that of Europeans. Their suffering is less because they are another, lesser kind of human – just as the suffering and pain of enslaved and colonised people were less important than the need to expand and enrich the citizens of Europe and settler col-oniser cousins.

How else can we understand the motivation to confine asylum seekers from Africa, Asia, and the Caribbean to processing cen-tres in Rwanda or barges off the coast of Britain, while at the same time British people are being encouraged to welcome Ukrainian refugees into their homes and communities? Why is their suffer-ing different? Why do their children deserve a home and safety when others in the same situation or worse do not?

The invisibility of the refugee, asylum-seeking mother

Within all this, where is the figure of the refugee or asylum-seeking mother? She is made invisible by the discourse of the illegal migrant who is overwhelmingly cast as young, male, and

Muslim – and therefore potentially a terrorist. She is consigned to the margins of civic and political life as she has no entitlement to the privileges of citizenship until she has "proved" her genuineness – a process which can take years. If she fails this test, she is forever illegal, subject to arrest and removal. If she "succeeds", where will she get the help and support anyone would need to finally feel safe and rebuild her and her children's lives in a new country following possible years of near destitution after making it here – to "safety"?

Black feminist thought has provided insight and analysis which has highlighted processes that are hidden or neglected by other scholarship. The work of writers like Sylvia Wynter (1990), Hortense Spillers (Spillers, 1987), and Nadine El Enany (2020) highlight the role of Black feminism in creating theory which recognises both the specificity of location and time, and also the commonalities of our experiences across time and space

Research which highlights how race and gender intersect to structure the experience of these women who are caught in the crossfire of powerful forces that challenge their very right to exist in the United Kingdom as fully human is the kind of scholarship that is important for me to carry out as a Black feminist in the academy. Drawing on contemporary Black feminist and critical race research, I want to both create new knowledge which gives voice to the silenced and also to privilege the work of other Black scholars, to help to redefine who is seen as possessing and creating expert knowledge.

The concerns of White feminist researchers do not always encompass the full range of our experiences and issues, such as the gender pay gap, body image, and media representation, which are all of our concerns but very often from a different perspective. Our lived experience of being both racialised and gendered "others" means that I am also concerned with wider issues of racial justice. As a mother of two Black children, I am equally affected by racism in schools and police violence, and as a member of the European diaspora and a second-generation immigrant, I am still deeply connected to the concerns of men and women "back home". Within the body of feminist scholarship, our concerns are still under-researched, and research on issues like violence and motherhood are often covered in ways which do not reflect our perspectives, or else portray us as victims of backward and repressive cultures from which we require saving (Emejulu and Sobande, 2019).

Black feminism post-Covid-19

So, what does it mean to be a Black feminist now in the 2020s? Have things changed so much that the ideas and concepts encapsulated by the Combahee declaration are less relevant today than they were in the 1970s and 1980s? The Covid-19 pandemic shone a light on the stark inequalities which shape the experiences and life chances of people who are poor, disabled, who are migrants or refugees, and who are people of colour across Europe and the United States and beyond. It highlighted the role of female and Black and migrant workers in badly paid and often insecure employment in providing essential public services and care to the most vulnerable, and how this in turn, alongside poor housing and poverty, increased their risk of serious illness and death. If proof was required of the need for intersectional theory and scholarship to understand and address how class, race, and gender-based oppression intersect, this surely must be it.

Watching George Floyd being murdered by so-called law enforcement officers in broad daylight on a busy street in Minneapolis, Minnesota (USA), the disgraceful stripping of British citizenship from Shamima Begum, and the gunning down of Chris Kaaba on a UK street minutes from my home brought forth memories of our previous struggles and leads me to conclude that we now live in similar troubled times where racism, misogyny, homophobia, and populist nationalism is on the rise worldwide. Within Western Europe and North America, this is seen most clearly in the increased violence by which borders are both enforced and extended – in the form of violence against people of colour, whether it is the killing of unarmed Black men in the United States or in the United Kingdom, by the police. The systematic denial of the very means of survival to refugees which is enshrined in UK law, or the reminder provided by the Begum case that our "acceptance" as British is conditional, is never certain if we are not White. Childhood, like personhood and citizenship, is not fully given to girls like Shamima Begum or the child she gave birth to who died in a refugee camp due to the refusal of the British government to allow her to return home. She was 15 when she joined Daesh – a child groomed online by adults and then married to an adult man. She was also born in the United Kingdom, and was supposedly a British citizen – what else except the continued process of dehumanisation based on racial ordering which has its roots in imperialism can explain why she was not seen as a victim of child abuse? If a White child had been groomed by a far-right group, would she have been demonised in the same way? Did any of the White female Members of Parliament who spoke out against the grooming of vulnerable White girls by Asian men speak up for her – and if not, why?

Black men killed by the police did not provoke outrage among the White activists who protested in force when a serving police officer raped and murdered Sarah Everard. Why is her life more important than that of Chris Kaba? Or indeed, why did the same people not rise in outrage when two Black women, Biba Henry and Nicole Smallman, murdered in London, had their images shared and ridiculed by the very officers whose job it was to find their killer and protect their dignity in death?

In 2023, we were being told that racism is receding because a multimillionaire banker who happens to be Asian became the prime minister of Britain, and the most enthusiastic government advocates of state-sanctioned violence are men and women of colour. We, like Sunak/Braverman/Patel Badenoch, who have the privileges of citizenship all, are all being invited to show our loyalty, to prove we deserve to belong by endorsing and supporting the politics of hate and division. Like Mirza (2015), I reject the idea that we live in "post-racial" times and argue Black feminist theory still offers us a framework to critically reflect, resist, organise, and build solidarity across boundaries. Her analysis that the "colour line" still exists talks back to the discourse that just because some of us have "made it" means that racism no longer exists.

By paying attention to not only race and gender but also class, we can see how hollow this argument is. It is also no accident that much of the discourse on gender advanced by Black women in government like Braverman and Badenoch is deeply homophobic and transphobic. Black feminist theory allows us to see this for what it is – an attempt to mobilise reactionary and morally conservative forces across all the communities of the United Kingdom in the service of a neoliberal economic agenda.

Conclusion

Leadership lessons in Black feminism and the work of the Combahee River Collective (1977) have demonstrated to me the uniqueness of Black feminism in inspiring change. My *"lived experience"* has been important in my involvement in decolonising initiatives in higher education, and this has further inspired my own research into mothering and refugee women. I have combined critical race theory themes in my approaches designed to amplify a leading role for Black feminist research in higher education. The fact that a new generation of Black feminist/womanist activists (Burkhard, 2022; Evans-Winters, 2019) is creating theory which draws attention to the continued and enduring power of Whiteness and coloniality gives me inspiration and hope. Black feminist theory is as relevant today as it was 40 or 50 years ago – as we see the hard-won gains we campaigned for in decolonising attempts in higher education. For changes in law and policy to occur, and to challenge sexist homophobic, racist violence and to promote accountability within public institutions, (be they schools, unions, or the police being rolled back in response to the so-called war on terror), Black feminism is needed more than ever.

We are now able to draw on the work of Black women academics who are both expanding and questioning the scope of Black feminism and examining issues such as transphobia and migration from an intersectional perspective. Nadine El Enany's (2020) work on law and bordering in twenty-first-century Britain is a powerful example of this. Such research provides us with a comprehensive analysis of how the policies of successive governments have continued to use the rhetoric and legal frameworks developed to support imperial expansion, to create a space of "domestic colonisation" where the benefits of citizenship for the few exist alongside the exclusion and continued marginalisation of the many. The politics discourse and government policy on refugee and asylum espoused by the current UK government is a stark example of this.

In her work *Feminism, Interrupted*, Lola Olufemi (2020) deploys the intersectional analysis outlined by Crenshaw (2006) and Collins (2000) to ask the question "Transmisogyny: who wins?" and to examine gendered Islamophobia. Her warning that the use of the category "woman" as fixed and exclusionary only serves to "distract our attention from the structures which determine the conditions of our lives and most importantly ensure that all women are not free" (p. 66), is a powerful reminder of the contemporary relevance of and enduring inspiration that Black feminist theory has and continues to provide.

In summary, I would argue that we are living in increasingly hostile times where racism, misogyny, and homo- and transphobia continue to be seen as acceptable and, in some spaces, normal and desirable – this is demonstrated in stark terms by the treatment of refugees in the United Kingdom and public discourse surrounding this. It may appear that we are fighting a losing battle – we must not lose hope, or be persuaded that what we believe as Black feminists is outdated and irrelevant. In fact, the opposite is true: the tools we have developed over more than 50 years allow us to analyse, organise, and challenge the contemporary formations of power which are fuelling division, hatred, and inequality in the twenty-first century. Within the academy, to identify as a Black feminist or womanist is to be committed to "teaching with love" and to producing theory which is both methodologically challenging of the status quo, and which contributes to wider struggles for social justice. We must both "be different" and "do different" if we are to achieve this. To thrive and survive in the academy while doing so, it is crucial that we develop and sustain systems to support and care for each other.

The next chapter turns to examining the role that Black women play as social justice activists, supporting decolonising programmes for social justice and mental well-being. The chapter explores the experiences of those Black women who continue to show up, the nature of their survival skills, and the ways that they deliver successful decolonising outcomes.

Learning objective

Understand the relationship between Black feminist research and the higher education decolonising programme.

7

Black feminist practice in decolonising for social justice and well-being

Jan Etienne, Yasmin Adan, and Nataliah Douglas

In promoting an ethic of care which is fit for purpose, our enduring mission is embedded in a belief that social justice and Black feminist practice can become prominent and permanent features of a new, carefully constructed, decolonising agenda in higher education. In such scenarios, the voices of the Black female are both heard and valued.

We begin our deliberations citing the words of the late Bonnie Candia-Bailey, a Black, female academic administrator, and vice president of student affairs at Lincoln University (Missouri, USA), who committed suicide in January 2024. The day before she died, she wrote: "You intentionally harassed and bullied me and got satisfaction from sitting back to determine how you would ensure I failed as an employee and proud alumna" (Weissman, 2024).

Let's take a moment to breathe.

In focusing on the informal mentoring roles carried out by Black women in education, we acknowledge that we ourselves are overburdened with responsibilities and many of us are going far beyond our day-to-day duties (Maylor, 2020) to pursue justice and equality for all. In so doing, it could be said that we are working as agents for decolonisation and our positions are forever compromised.

It is time for change, and we call for an examination and the use of an ethic of care (Collins, 2000) by the mainstream. How can social justice approaches as outlined in Black feminist thought help to develop and sustain good mental health and well-being in the education academy? We can all deliver an ethic of care; however, in practice, raising the voices of Black women is seldom a reality.

As Black female teachers and researchers, in this work, we call for personal accountability and draw on themes arising from our own qualitative research studies, and reveal our efforts as social justice activists, committed to delivering decolonising programmes in higher education. This chapter celebrates a call for global social justice and places a Black feminist lens on the education academy and its decolonising attempts to improve mental health and well-being for all. In revealing the social justice narratives of Black women in education, we show the ways in which decolonising activism is carried out on the margins of the education institution. As teachers and researchers of Black feminist thought, we strive to embody social justice approaches across our pedagogy, and it is central not only to our academic discipline but also to the way we navigate our daily lives. To speak anecdotally is perhaps the only way to describe the centrality of social justice work in higher education.

Reflecting largely on the thinking of Evans-Winters (2019), Daley (2020), Mathibela (2020), Collins (2000), and Mirza, (1997), we contend that there are still power dynamics operating today which deny Black women opportunities to freely speak out and have their voices heard. Such dynamics can be seen in anti-decolonising sentiments occurring in strategies which appear helpful but reinforce negative stereotypes and microaggressions. We argue that existing social justice efforts to address issues of inequality in education are largely performative and exist only to maintain the status quo. Throughout this work, when we speak of activism, we speak of social justice and decolonising work in higher education.

As teachers and researchers of Black feminist thought, we strive to embody social justice approaches across our pedagogy, and it is central not only to our academic discipline but also to the way we navigate our daily lives. For some of us in the United Kingdom, decolonising was at the height of the RhodesMustFall campaign during our undergraduate studies where university campuses across the world were set alight with the fervour to decolonise the academy. Here, peers, tutors, and lecturers from all backgrounds and interests were suddenly engulfed in the call to decolonise the university. Although, it was a call to confront the realities of the university as a space that continued to legitimise the violence of Whiteness, the experience for us and other Black women who were students, peers, researchers, and teachers was that these were the conversations, grievances, and shared realities we had been confronting for years. Suddenly, the decolonial cause had gained momentum and universities were forced to respond. Although Black and other marginalised communities were used or rather tokenised to fulfil the quota on inclusion in conversations and campaigns, to address the rage, all too often Black women were once again left to be made invisible, or rather hypervisible.

Black women's activism, although widespread, continues to be undertheorised in educational research. Mirza (1997) points out that Black women have been viewed within the dominant discourse as oppressed and "least visible" (p. 276). Additionally, she recognises that Black female agency remains invisible in the masculinist discourse of "race" and social change (Mirza, 1997, p. 272). Our invisibility within social justice work and activism has traditionally been erased from histories. Mathibela (2020) highlights the erasure of women's contributions within postcolonial struggles and suggests that the birth of the nation state ensured that women were erased to make way for the "boys club" (p. 130). That strategic erasure of Black women's contribution to social justice work mirrors the masculinist framing of social change which is confrontational, visible, and radical (Collins, 1990). Mathibela (2020) highlights similar sentiments from Black women who were involved in the emancipatory struggle for freedom in South Africa and notes that women felt their activism had been censored "rather than made clearly visible in male-dominated literary communities, policy development and liberation history" (p. 123).

Opening up marginalised voices

Theorists such as hooks (1994) acknowledge the importance of opening up marginalised voices and suggest the occupants of the margin offer a space of radical possibility and change "where alternative realities and new worlds are imagined" (p. 341). Adopting Black feminist principles of care and love in realising the need for spaces to talk, to nurture sisterly support as we recover ourselves is highly necessary.

The new energy for decolonising work in education across the UK education sectors is partly as a result of global events, such as Black Lives Matter post the murder of George Floyd (Solomon and Ehlinger, 2023). This has produced a complex discourse in relation to social justice within the academy. By utilising a Black feminist lens, we are able to delve into the nature of everyday acts of resistance, healing, rage, and joy that are often invisible and personalised, in decolonial practices in education. We argue that social justice is Black feminist, and Black women carry this in their minds and take action to address incidents of inequality as and when they see it played out in their day-to-day lives. Thinking Black feminist is highly necessary to survive higher education but at what cost to the individual Black female activist?

It was because our conversations and experiential knowledge were not valued and our activism did not "fit" the activism of the neoliberal university, that our voices were denied, not heard, not considered relevant. However, amidst the momentum of the call to decolonise, the hypervisibility of Black women became apparent. Here we were thrown into spaces where we were called upon and demanded to perform. Subsequently, the same epistemological violence that Black female students faced prior to the rise in the decolonial efforts, had become exacerbated and Black female teachers became targets with the responsibility to deliver change. Our views were sought after, regularly, time and time again, mulled over in seminars and workshops but seldom used to promote change. The degradation of Black women emerged at an early age, used and abused and discarded over time.

The adultification of Black girls

As higher education educators and researchers, we regard our social justice strategies as key in making things better for ourselves and others. We act together in our quiet campaigning groups to defend each other and believe it necessary, as a starting point, to examine issues in the schools sector and, in particular, the adultification of Black girls, where "Black and global majority children are held to adult standards, and where their white peers are less likely to be" (Hackney Council, 2022). In the United Kingdom in this regard, a highly publicised safeguarding report, involving "Child Q", concluded that racism was likely to be an "influencing factor" in the strip-search of a Black female child – who was subjected to "adultification". In such a serious scenario, the young Black female is often perceived not as youthful but as older and more self-reliant, leading to reduced recognition of her need for mental health support and other forms of assistance.

> Child Q was subjected to humiliating, traumatising and utterly shocking treatment by police officers – actions that were wholly disproportionate to the alleged incident to which they had been called. This is exacerbated

by the fact that the strip search was carried out at school – a place where the child had an expectation of safety, security and care. Instead, she was let down by those who were meant to protect her. (Hackney Council, 2022)

How should we analyse and take an interest in the conversations of Black women in response to adultification and its impact? To what extent is this type of treatment and lack of respect for Black girls replicated in other areas of education? In the absence of safe spaces that allow for authentic and purposeful conversations to manifest, the decolonial project became co-opted by the values and confines of neoliberal university norms. There is no formal space to freely facilitate Black feminist discussion as the demands placed on our professional lives mean we have little opportunity to speak out, together and with purpose. Black women are systematically excluded from academic discourses within mainstream education policy and practice, despite our valuable contributions. Intersectionality is often either misunderstood or entirely ignored. Decolonial projects frequently fail to create space—both physical and theoretical—for Black women, with our efforts dismissed as too radical or simply misunderstood by the predominantly White male academic body. As a result, Black women are often left isolated, vulnerable, and without a voice.

Black feminism and activism

It becomes critical then to deploy a Black feminist lens when exploring the activism and decolonial efforts of Black women across education. The decolonial efforts of Black women are rooted in our daily lives, and our efforts are often centred in confrontational scenarios that we recognise, and that are not always necessary for our own well-being and survival within the academy. We confront racist policies, interactions, microaggressions, and norms within higher education which are often dismissed as minor inconveniences. Supporting each other and confronting injustice in our communities are the ways in which Black women in higher education have historically been able to survive.

To overcome, and flourish in the violence of the academy, Black women seek safe spaces through the interactions, joy, and shared realities of Black womanhood in solidarity. The stories we tell, and the support and community we inhabit in an effort to overcome the systemic violence perpetuated against us need to be understood. Outside these protective spaces, we as Black women are made to feel that we have no significant contribution to make to decolonial efforts.

What is decolonising for well-being in higher education?

Decolonising can take a plethora of forms and practices, from curriculum change and mentoring to sensitising well-being practices. As universities faced the pressure to demonstrate solidarity with the wider decolonial movement there came about various initiatives and stances on how to do this. Although popular discussions on decolonising higher education are largely associated with the removal of racist imperialist figures from university campuses, whether here in the United Kingdom or in South Africa, decolonial struggle in the university is often rooted in confrontation centred around replacing or removing existing histories and deradicalising decolonial efforts to review curricula and focus on diversity. Too often, the impact of racism on the mental health and well-being of Black students and Black staff is ignored by the education sector. Strategies which take account of race discrimination and its impact are carried out by Black and other ethnic minority students and academics through free labour. These Black students and teaching staff all too often face hostile challenges in their efforts.

It is critical to note, then, that decolonising the university is about confronting the university as a space that reproduces knowledge rooted in imperialist values as well as a space that rejects plurality. In all attempts to brand universities as spaces of radical change and innovation, this is disappointingly far from the truth due to the silencing and framing of those outside of a White habitus which is not considered credible sources of knowledge production. Despite the framing of decolonising projects to fit an acceptable narrative, universities can still remain spaces where radical change happens (Daley, 2020).

Social justice strategies in higher education

Social justice strategies in education have been explored by educators and theorists for decades (Bryan et al., 1985; Daley, 2020; Freire, 1970; hooks, 1994), and the revival of social justice within the British education system in the United Kingdom has resulted in both direct and indirect attempts at challenging systems of oppression. The unified dedication to social justice, however, presents its own challenges. Social justice remains an abstract concept. However, there is no recognition beyond social media references and exaggerated political news headlines which create space and allow the authentic voices of Black female activist teachers to be heard. Universities are given the spotlight purposefully to detract from the possibility of a discourse on alternative forms of activism and the quest for social justice inside the education academy.

For too long there has been a refusal to frame "Black women as producers of knowledge, and a tradition of racial and gender exclusion" (Evans-Winters, 2019, p. 16) has been permitted to exist. Largely, this is due in part to the fact that qualitative methods are restrictive and devalue Black women's intellectual thought. According to feminist qualitative researchers, Black women's expression and ways of being are not valued. That sense of urgency requires adopting a different approach to deploying Black female narratives to ensure their experiences are authentically represented and valued (Etienne, 2016). There is a lack of space within both the physical and the theoretical educational arena for Black female teachers to express their activism outside of regulated institutions. Additionally, we take the issue that decolonising the curriculum is a central and much under-researched challenge faced by the education institution. Our research seeks to open up safe spaces for Black women to speak authentically and to show up without leaving any part of ourselves behind. Our narratives are central to exploring alternative possibilities because of our position at the intersection of race and gender (hooks, 1990). There is a need to address projects in contemporary contexts that attempt to dehumanise, oppress, suppress, and annihilate Black bodies. Not only is there a need to create spaces within academic institutions and social justice movements, but also to challenge contemporary constructions of social justice work. Black feminist thought (Collins, 2000) assists us in exploring the ways in which working alongside and theorising with Black women can reveal "Black women's commitment to challenging racism and sexism" as rooted in their lived experience as Black women (Evans-Winters, 2019, p. 16), thus, signifying the long-standing tradition of Black women's commitment to social justice work.

Despite the obstacles faced by teachers and students as hooks (2003) notes, the classroom remains the space where revolutionary and radical change is possible. A sense of duty and personal accountability (Collins, 2000) urges Black female teachers to ensure we carry out care and inspire their students. hooks (2003) suggests "Hopefulness empowers us to continue our work for justice even as the forces of injustice may gain greater power for a time. As teachers we enter the classroom with hope" (p. 15).

Within a British context, Patricia Daley (2020) states that "Black British women's feminism has received little attention" (p. 24). The invisibility of Black women has been countered more recently through the Black Lives Matter (BLM) movement and other diagonal grassroots movements, and women's contributions to activism have become more visible. Cecile Wright (2005) echoes these sentiments as she suggests that Black women in BLM reflect their "long history as key players in movements for social justice" (2005 p. 50). Thus, the global expansion of BLM mirrors a long-standing culture for activism and social justice work.

Black women's activism in social justice approaches impacting well-being

Black women's activism in Britain can be seen as "catalysts for societal and institutional change that inspire both healing and transformation" (Wright, 2005, p. 51). Black supplementary schools are an example of social justice work carried out overwhelmingly by Black women (Mirza 1997), and this reflects the way in which Black women's activism is represented as miniscule and conformist where these schools are radical spaces which offer "alternative worlds, ways of knowing" (Mirza, 1997, p. 272). Community organisation play a "central role in informal well-being programmes, minimising the impact of social exclusion on young Black people" in particular (Reynolds, 2008, p. 55). Mirza (1997) suggests that "Black supplementary schools are an example of Black women evolving a system of strategic rationalization which has its own logic, values, and codes" (Mirza, 1997, p. 276). A key point to note is the discourse on Black women's activism demonstrating Black female identities as the subservient, self-sacrificing, caring mother (Evans-Winters, 2019; Williams, 1993; Wallace-Sanders, 2009). In this regard, we seek to contextualise not only the ways Black women's activism manifests in education, but how we resist these enforced prescriptions of self and identity. A central reason behind this approach, is to point out that our erasure from academia as both researchers and participants is largely due to the rigid frameworks which establish set power relations denying Black women voice. Narratives are not neutral and are always socially constrained forms of action, socially situated performances, ways of acting in, and making sense of the world. Thus, deploying narrative storytelling using principles of Black feminist thought, removes from a research an approach that has continuously represented Black women as victims (Evans-Winters, 2019). When teachers are invited to contribute to the discourse on education, the overwhelming under-representation of Black women in senior positions in the academy (Etienne, 2020) is not reassuring.

Narrative storytelling

Using narrative storytelling "provides counter stories to racist and patriarchal portrayal" (Evans-Winters, 2019, p. 22) of Black women. Simultaneously, this raises questions and challenges existing claims of Black women as uninterested or not credible sources of knowledge. In addition, the annihilation and erasure of Black women as researchers and participants also inspired the use of narrative storytelling as a methodological framework. Evans-Winters (2019) goes on to assert that the "lack of awareness of Black women as producers of knowledge, and a tradition of racial and gender exclusion in the academy" ensures that knowledge claims and knowledge production remain rooted in a White middle-class habitus that seeks to serve the interests and needs of White people.

Activism changes this position, as it is seen and organised, and, as Patricia Hill Collins (1990) suggests, the erasure of Black women's social justice work is often intertwined with the presumption that social change and social work are confrontational, visible, and radical. However, this framing of activism becomes contested as teachers are confined to the politics of a neoliberal framework as well as guidance and policies both on a local and a national level. Thus, their supposed activism becomes visible as it cannot be rendered true due to the enforced allegiance to a political system and our inability to act out in a confrontational and visible way when we are already vilified, marginalised, and under-represented (Wright, 2025). Black female teachers reflect an activism that challenges the masculine framework of social justice work. Our perception of activism describes acts that are rooted in their daily rituals and routines (Etienne, 2020).

Black women – showing up for activism

Black women described the act of "showing up" as activist work, as a way of "bringing their lived realities to the research context" (Evans-Winters, 2019, p. 17). Being a presence and teaching with a Black feminist ethic of care in the education setting can resist and defy the expectation of not only what is considered activism, but also a masculine framework of activist work. Black women are not charging the gates of the academy, marching, or holding placards. "Showing up" is an unapologetic manifestation of Black womanhood, femininity, and identity. Within activist work across educational sections, "Black women have felt the need to take on hypermasculine expressions in order to maintain a voice" (Mathibela, 2020, p. 128), discussing the experiences of Black women in higher education, and the ways in which we are made to feel inadequate and unable to authentically present ourselves (Lorde, 2015). We draw parallels with the challenges faced in the pursuit of activism and Black female leadership roles in academia. As Mirza (1997) argues, "for black women strategies of everyday survival consist of trying to create spheres of influence that are separate from but engaged with existing structures of oppression" (p. 276).

Black women showing up is not limited to the needs of their students; the sisterhood that comes from representation is a significant and critical part of the lives of all Black women. Patricia Daley (2020) highlights the importance of collectivity for the survival of Black women. For this reason, the representation of Black female activist teachers and educators remains a radical activist stance. For the students, seeing these women living their authentic lives and working within a violent system offers a much-needed source of inspiration, strength, and hope. As a collectivist stance, Black women 'showing up' mirrors Alice Walker's call for a 'theory/movement for the survival of the black women, black culture, black myths, spiritual life, and orality—femininity and culture are equally important to the woman's existence' (Walker, 1983, p. 27).

The exploration of social justice within education, then, goes beyond debates of curriculum representation and reveals a more complex discourse on how social justice is acted out from the activism of Black female teachers and educators.

Black women and a sense of responsibility

Black supplementary schools mirror the practical ways Black women are "doing the work" to establish social justice as well as the sense of duty and responsibility Black women feel. Mirza (1997) suggests:

> Black supplementary schools, as organic grassroots organizations, are not simply a response to mainstream educational exclusion and poor practice, as they are described. They are far more radical and subversive than their quiet conformist exterior suggests [...] the women, who were for the most part voluntary unpaid teachers, talked of their "joy" of what they do, "the gift of giving back", of their work to "raise the race". (p. 273)

Black women's activism is historically represented as a default state of being

What this tells us, then, is that for Black female teachers, a sense of responsibility underpins their activist roles, which are further rooted in a radical politics. Within a British context, Black supplementary schools exemplify the ways in which Black women engage in activism within systems of oppression that are continually reproduced; they find ways to flourish. However, due to the expectations of responsibility and freely given care, supplementary schools were long overlooked as radical spaces of transformation (Mirza, 1997).

Black female teachers' sense of responsibility and the ways in which we are "doing the work" as activists stems from our own experiences of prejudice and discriminatory actions in our education journey and in our careers. Activism then becomes a personal responsibility to allow healing and transformation not only for the students we work with but also ourselves. By pursuing a sense of personal responsibility, Black female teachers ensure they are breaking the cycle of violence that young Black people experience in the education system. Showing up as activists, then, is a way of speaking truths that are based on traumatic experiences within the lives of Black female teachers. As Audre Lorde (2019) suggests, there is a necessity to teach by living and speaking those truths which we believe and know beyond understanding "because in this way alone we can survive, by taking part in a process of life that is creative and continuing, that is growth (Lorde, 2019, p. 32).

Black women and representation

As Black feminist activists, we are mindful of looking out for the well-being of our students, and we know that carrying the responsibility of being a role model and a "first", whilst carefully managing the angry Black woman archetype, the feisty co-worker, is forever present. We also know that in our attempts to find ways to decolonise mental health support services, we are reminded that young Black girls are watching us.

Having high expectations of students, particularly Black boys who are not expected to do well, is a practical way we apply Black feminist principles in our social justice approaches. Although all teachers pledge to have high expectations of all students, historically, discriminatory views and actions (Wright, Maylor, and Pickup, 2021) are still occurring in British education settings.

In our research conversations with Black learners, one student told us: "A Black teacher is going to continuously challenge you, and push you mentally, emotionally, and you know is going to expect you to do the long hours to finish what you started."

Dialogue for Black students is not something freely committed; they also need safe spaces. Black female teachers recognise this, having ourselves, experienced the hostile environments within schooling and in our careers.

Black feminist approaches to collaboration

Collaboration is another way that Black female teachers describe doing the work of healing. As Mirza (1997) suggests,

> doing well can become a radical strategy. An act of social transformation. The black women educators did not accept the dominant discourse. In their space on the margin, they have evolved a system of strategic rationalization of the dominant discourse. They operate within, between, under, and alongside the mainstream educational and labour market structures, subverting, renaming and reclaiming opportunities for their children through their transformative pedagogy of "raising the race"– a radical pedagogy, that ironically appears conservative on the surface with its focus on inclusion and dialogue with the mainstream. (p. 274)

Mirza's reflection on academic excellence as a transformative approach mirrors the role of Black female secondary teachers. Their upholding standards for their students and ensuring their success, fulfilling their job description as teachers, reflects a radical stance. Their activism is the way in which Black women present their strategies working within the limitations of a rigid neoliberal school system. They work and live within the rhythm of their own lives (Etienne, 2020) alongside the mainstream educational and labour markets, and it is this delicate act of balancing that grounds the activism of black female teachers.

Importantly, the ways in which Black women are "doing the work" offers a new possibility for looking at social justice within education. There is no rigid criteria or formulas to follow, or a training programme that needs to be curated to practise social justice. The central requirement is a willingness to work towards dismantling systems of oppression (Freire, 1970; hooks, 1994) and encouraging critical thought, allowing students to realise their truth and fulfil their potential. The responses within the conversations, between instructor and students, are rooted in experiential knowledge of the pains of racism and sexism faced by Black female teachers. Social justice, then, becomes a commitment that goes beyond a verbal allegiance to listen and learn, to work by "any means necessary". What this also means is to recognise the differences and variations within our student body, within a neoliberal system that enforces a meritocratic system under the guise of equality. Black female teachers represent a pedagogy of hope (hooks, 2003) in which they work towards social justice because of their experiential knowledge. However, Black women are also aware of the dangers of their activist work as society inscribes care roles to their identities.

Who cares for us?

In *Their Eyes Were Watching God*, Nanny declares "de nigger woman is the de mule uh de world so fur as Ah can see" (Wallace-Sanders, 2009, p. 80). Nanny's declaration reflects the state of the Black woman as a self-sacrificing and maternal figure. Rooted in the "mammy" of the colonial period, the mammy loves the White child more than her own child and feels privileged to deliver care (Wallace-Sanders, 2009). Thus, Black women must care for others at their own expense. But who cares for us? Social justice is at the heart of our campaigns for change, and as Black women we continue to be seen as able to cope – that strong Black female trope is all powerful. The first Black British female MP, the Black British trailblazing politician and lawmaker Diane Abbot, endured decades of horrific racist and misogynistic abuse throughout her political life, yet she was triumphantly re-elected to the British Parliament in 2024. She remains strong and vigilant (Abbot, 2024). What lessons can we learn from her well-being experience?

Conclusion

We conclude, there is a violent impact of imposed expectations of care on Black female teachers. There is no doubt that we are dedicated to the challenge of promoting social justice within education and we do so freely. However, to overlook the impact of inscribing racist and sexist identities would be an act of injustice. To romanticise Black women's activism as desirable and commendable work without giving voice to the suffering and violence they experience, works to reinscribe the "mammy" image of the self-sacrificing Black woman. Social justice in decolonising work must become an institutional priority rather than a narrated performance. Acts of self-care then become a radical form of resistance against racist and sexist inscriptions of Black women's identities.

The trauma Black female teachers experience as hypervisible in a post-George Floyd world continues in the pursuit of an education system that reflects social justice. It is essential that Black female teachers, disproportionally affected by policy change and systemic violence, and their lived realities are not neglected. If these concerns are not taken seriously, then the very systems we seek to change become reproductive and transformation cannot occur. To reflect, masking alienation, in addition to succumbing to the pressure to succeed in fulfilling parental expectations, whilst potentially downplaying or ignoring their own talent in order to avoid bias towards the "aggressive/angry Black woman/ adultification" can impact Black female teachers' mental health in the long term. However, because institutions already have an unconscious or conscious adultification bias towards young women, interventions may be missed. Usually, professionals can identify behaviours or symptoms linked to mental ill-health, particularly for young White women. Young Black women are expected to manage on their own. If they are unable to do so, it is seen as deserved or as their bringing it upon themselves due to being aggressive and uncooperative.

There is complexity surrounding pastoral care in education, and the shift from secondary to higher education. As a form of a triple shift that uniquely applies to Black women in British secondary education, the role of Safeguarding Lead, or Pastoral Lead is solely given to them. In most cases, Black female educators are expected to take on this role, without pay or formal acknowledgement because of our perceived "nurturing" disposition. Whilst this care is denied to young Black females in secondary education, in higher education, the caring, nurturing pastoral team is no longer present Young Black female learners are moulded to be hard workers who know how to navigate the system and manage their mental health in safe spaces. However, they often find themselves starting over, trying to establish their place, while simultaneously contending with microaggressions and filtering through layers of institutional racism. Their mental health becomes second to last in priority.

This chapter explored and examined the centrality of social justice and decolonial work impacting the Black female educator, through experiences in British secondary education to higher education. We argue the centrality of initiatives to decolonise the education curriculum by theorising the activism of Black female teachers. We believe there has been a concerted effort by those in power, both locally and nationally, to shield the academy from the influence of movements advocating for social justice. Despite the mass silencing of students and the censorship within the academy, the resilience and fearlessness of the students and teachers who continue to stand against systems of domination in the face of undeniable epistemological and physical violence continue to inspire us. Social justice is an institutional priority in today's higher education.

The next chapter discusses our approaches to collaboration for decolonising and for intersectionality and change.

Learning objective

Understand the nature of Black feminist approaches to an ethic of care and personal accountability in decolonising work in higher education.

Conclusion

Closing remarks

8
Decolonisation, intersectionality, and change

Black and decolonial feminist collaboration

Jan Etienne and Tanja Burkhard

In 2003, Hortense Spillers wrote: "My discomfort remains lodged, however in academic feminism's shaky relationship to 'race' matters, or more specially, the truncation of its sense of social justice across the boundaries of the provincial" (p. 12). This final quote from the pen of Black feminist scholar Hortense Spillers remains at the forefront of our thinking as we conclude our deliberations on feminist scholars' approaches to decolonising the higher education academy. In exposing our beliefs and ways of doing decolonising work in the academy, we acknowledge the feminist scholar's dedication to challenging the absence of a genuine presence for issues impacting Black women in the mainstream feminist discourse. The position of "race" is therefore paramount in a discourse of feminist approaches to decolonising the academy.

Our earlier chapters revealed a desire to see the academy upholding principles of social justice (Daley, 2020) and confronting race and sex discrimination in the context of an understanding of intersectionality (Haynes et al., 2021) and the multiple layers of discriminatory practices impacting the lives of Black women and other marginalised groups of women. Some of us may argue that taking action to address inequalities in respect to race and gender makes understandings of all other forms of oppression that much clearer. However, in moving forward, we recognise that our decolonising project in higher education must prioritise all feminist voices in a collaborative effort to deliver change together.

As the authors writing these closing reflections, we are located in different parts of the world, where we are confronted with social justice issues that do not always occur simultaneously. However, at the same time, we share the same mission in a desire for collaborative work to elevate the voices of women who are missing from the discussion on the practical implementation of decolonising work in higher education. We are stronger together when involved in the debate to introduce new strategies to improve representation, and in finding ways to address such critical issues as closing the attainment gap and other major equity and diversity concerns in higher education. One area of our research specialisms is Womanism and another is transnational Black feminisms. In both areas, we are involved in using qualitative methodologies with intersectionality as a primary engagement. In earlier chapters in this volume, we observed how contributors navigated educational spaces with intersectionality in mind, as they revealed the challenges they faced in their enthusiasm to make decolonising the academy a reality. We ourselves acknowledged the nature of social justice at the centre of our work and noted the intersections of race, gender, class, sexuality, identity, and disability discrimination creating additional challenges for us as we navigate the social world. In our Black feminist research practice, we see how intersectionality (Collins, 2019; Crenshaw, 2014; Nash, 2019) has become ubiquitous and a widely accepted concept. Drawing on data from a qualitative research study of the lived experiences of Black immigrant women educators, we have interrogated intersectionality as a dominant concept in the context of decolonial feminist research practice in higher education and in consideration of transnational, Black, and decolonial feminist epistemologies. But we are aware of the complexities and multiple dimensions at play when we consider the global structures that shape Black women's lives (Avtar Brah, 1996).

We have challenged each other to think through difference in the academy whilst producing and working alongside each other, towards not just solidarity but also intimacy and knowledge production. In that way, we think there are a few great examples of making these collaborative efforts work. We appreciate that this moves us away from hyperindividualised ways of thinking about research and of thinking about knowledge, but ultimately, it's where we would like to see more work emerge, less of one name on one paper claiming all this knowledge, and instead truly thinking, writing, and analysing with each other. So, we have appreciated putting the idea of solidarity into action in the writing of this volume. It is of course at times important to have a single-author focus, but that does not always align with our epistemology, and it is not necessarily the theories that we draw from as decolonial feminist scholars. This collaboration, individual but together, is a good example of how we should continue to move beyond these boundaries.

In our discussions around intersectionality methodology and how it might be utilised in moving a decolonising project in higher education forward, contributors spent a great deal of time thinking about this. We respond to questions such as: Do you need to be Black to think Black feminist? The answer is clearly no. Does the researcher have to be or identify as feminist or female? Today, we have a much more robust articulation of what it means to be a Black feminist researcher and what it means to use intersectionality. In this volume, we show that we are not all from the same class background, although many of us are. We have had very different experiences, and even though some of our racialised and gendered experiences may have been similar, further discussion in some areas can be a case for growth and it cannot happen without in-depth collective conversations. Questioning our own assumptions about what it means to work alongside each other and what it means to reclaim some of these ideas that have been used to subjugate us, is important, not least in order to work towards transformation and change.

We recently engaged with work by Heidi Mirza (2014) that talked about the fact that from 1995 a number of Black women leaders have been held up as examples of trailblazing and pathfinding changemakers who carry responsibility on their shoulders due to their success in leadership. However, this form of representation reflects a masculinist and capitalist perspective on success and its impact. In contrast, Mirza encourages us to focus on the every-day transformations and work carried out by Black women. This work often goes unrecognized, uncelebrated, and unrewarded with traditional success stories, yet it is through these efforts that meaningful change is truly pioneered and made possible. As such, we consider the small conversations, the additional time spent, the support provided, and how we can reshape ourselves to continue being honest about pursuing a collectivist vision, even when this individualised and masculine lens continues to be imposed on us.

The suicide of Dr Antoinette Candia Bailey in the United States, a Black woman leader at a historically Black institution, is a damn-ing indictment of the professional circumstances in which many Black women find themselves in higher education settings. Dr Bailey's students, colleagues, and fellow women in academia talked about her warm and supportive nature, the fact that she attended doctoral defences, and showed up for presentations and other events when her support was needed. They talked about the pressure of being a Black woman in academia with a steadily increasing workload as she worked towards change at her institution. Dr Bailey's tragic example made us think again about what it means to be in relation with each other, to work towards this collective idea, to become professional sapphires (Haynes et al., 2021) that push back against mental harm and damage.

As Black feminists, we advocate for a decolonial feminism that addresses the complex, interwoven systems of oppression shap-ing social identities—such as race, class, gender, sexuality, and disability—to challenge and dismantle dominant, harmful ideologies in higher education. In this book, we have demonstrated the nature of decolonising work carried out by a group of activist researchers and academics committed to a decolonial feminist higher education agenda which allows the voices of minority women to be heard. Voice and collaboration are acknowledged in the contributions of others as we concur that "Black feminist ways of thinking is activism" (Nayak, 2015, pp. 204), and in pursuing our realisation of this notion, we allow ourselves to acknowledge a shared approach to owning a social problem – that of the absence of voice. As Audre Lorde (1980) declared "Black feminism is not feminism with a different face" (1980, p. 34). It must be understood with all its layers of significance and unique complexities.

Collectively, we have acknowledged the ways in which we can promote practical understandings of Black feminist theory as a useful tool in helping to address critical social issues and develop anti-racist, decolonising agendas in higher education. We explore tutor identity in helping to deliver effective anti-racist, decolonising strategies in higher education, encouraging ways in which we can share good practice in using Black feminist theories and the usefulness of tutor identity. We explore the significance of class, tutor, and sexual identity in helping to deliver effective anti-racist, decolonising programmes in higher education. The volume encourages leadership and delivery of Black feminist approaches to shaping anti-racist, decolonising programmes in higher education.

In conclusion, we restate: Black feminist theory as a form of being in the world, as "somebody's daughter", allows us not only to understand our interconnection with the world around us, but also to concern ourselves with the responsibility and accountability for our actions, specifically to those who care about us (Reynolds, 2008) and "claim us as members of their community and those who came before us" (Burkhard, 2022 p. 19). We have explored intersectionality and ways of decolonising class-based practice to decolonise approaches to teaching practice, and call on the academy to adopt a similar way of thinking in its approach to tackling issues such as representation in higher education. We emphasise how Black feminist theory is already being used in the academy and make close connections with the theme of "Voice" adopted in our own Black feminist qualitative studies. We acknowledge the use of "an ethic of care" in anti-racist policy and practice. After the "Summer of Racial Reckoning" in the United States, we noted an experience of severe discomfort in the classroom, which led one of us to ask: what does it mean to teach social justice when learners are suffering? "How do such situations impact Black tutors?". Here, we draw on our own work using Black feminist theory in autoethnographic strategies to examine racialised, gendered, and xenophobic incidents in classes focused on equality and diversity.

This book discussed Kimberlé Crenshaw's work (1989) on intersectionality to explain the nature of oppression in the approach to student identities and educational experiences, allowing for the contextualisation of historical and contemporary factors to be understood. The work of Heidi Mirza (2018) was used to illustrate decolonising challenges in discussions of "colonialism, empire and racism" by exploring how these discourses continue to permeate contemporary society. Whilst for some, decolonisation may appear to be simply paying lip service to already existing issues surrounding racial injustice, it has meant that some higher education institutions are now focusing more intensely on equality, diversity, and inclusion (EDI) issues such as the degree awarding gap. However, the authors argue that genuine work on closing the attainment gap cannot be separated from the decolonising agenda. We believe that a Black feminist perspective has a critical role to play in making higher education EDI policies fit for purpose. By bringing together the reflective narratives of decolonial anti-racist feminist tutors and researchers (diverse in race and gender identities), we have been determined to show how Black feminist theory can help deliver Equality and Diversity strategies, and at the same time, promote race equality and inclusion in contested spaces inside higher education.

Drawing on their lived experiences, the contributors to this volume use a Black feminist, postcolonial feminist lens to shine a light on the usefulness of Black feminist thought in helping to meet equality and diversity strategies in their respective higher education practices. The authors foreground unlawful killings of Black youths in Britain and in the United States to demonstrate how social injustices in the global north have brought feminist educators together to improve the effectiveness of existing decolonising initiatives in higher education. In our deliberations we have related closely to the discussion and themes under study, seeking to prompt senior management to adopt an ethic of care in their "ownership" of the workings of Black feminist theory principles. In the words of Audre Lorde, it is time to "negotiate difference" in the university's hierarchy.

Black feminist voices in higher education serve as a compelling development, helping to deliver diversity commitments and making decolonising the academy initiatives fit for purpose. We call for anti-racist decolonial feminists beyond this publication, to hold institutions to account by adopting alternative approaches to tackling long-standing concerns impacting Black learners and staff. This book is a road map for change as it shines a light on the usefulness of Black feminist theory in helping to carry out equality and diversity strategies in higher education. We argue that such key work helps to counter what Ahmed (2017) refers to as "White men: a citational relation". Those working within the academy must also consider the ways academic knowledges are produced (and reproduced) to provide more expansive and less parochial ways of knowing and understanding the world. Black feminist theory allows opportunities to reimagine our approaches by considering our personal accountability to shape our agendas and introduce measures that are grounded in an ethic of care in the neoliberal UK higher education sector.

In studying Black feminist theory, we bring into focus critical social concerns, and introduce Black feminist approaches to an urgent area of higher education diversity policy and practice. Black feminist voices in higher education serve as a compelling development, helping to deliver diversity commitments and making decolonising the academy initiatives fit for purpose. We acknowledge that those higher education institutions that are motivated and committed to rethinking the areas addressed in this volume, to identifying sustainable strategies to decolonise the academy are best placed to achieve successful outcomes for all learners.

Recommended assignments/ Discussion questions

- Chapter 1: How far can decolonial feminism assist us in bringing feminist voices together to tackle institutional change in decolonising higher education?

- Chapter 2: What is the value of Black feminist text in the higher education curriculum?

- Chapter 3: How do we build on widening participation and access programmes to develop decolonising activities in higher education?

- Chapter 4: How can visual arts-based approaches inspired by Black feminist thought, help demystify the decolonising programme in higher education?

- Chapter 5: How can senior management in higher education include Black feminist approaches in their day-to-day work to help improve diversity and inclusion outcomes?

- Chapter 6: What is the relationship between Black feminist research and the higher education decolonising programme?

- Chapter 7: How might Black feminist principles in an *ethic of care* help to decolonise everyday well-being practices in higher education practice?

- Chapter 8: What lessons can the British higher education sector learn from a US-dominated Black feminist academic discourse in their efforts to decolonise the higher education academy?

Other assignments

- To what extent are Black female teachers carrying out decolonising work as part of their day-to-day duties? What messages do they have for the higher education sector?

- To what extent are Black female teachers carrying out decolonising work as part of their day-to-day duties? What lessons do they have for the higher education sector?

- How can identity and lived experience be critically evaluated in the context of decolonising the academy?

- What is the role of decolonising pedagogy in challenging intersectional discrimination within the neoliberal university, and how can it be critically evaluated?

- As a practitioner, how might you apply the ethos of bell hooks' understanding of "care of the soul"?

Notes

Chapter 2

1. Brazilian poem and song which portray there is not just one story but there are lots of stories in one.

2. Candomblé is an oral culture with no sacred text. There are seven Candomblé nations, such as Ketu and Angola, depending on where in Africa the slaves practising it came from. We believe in a supreme being, called Olódùmarè. Beneath this God there are 16 Orixás, many of whom have characteristics that are distinctly human in nature.

3. I was born in Brazil, which was one of the last countries to abolish slavery. Brazil was the country which had the largest number of Black people outside the African continent. At the beginning of the nineteenth century, Brazil had a population of 3,818,000 people, of whom 1,930,000 were slaves.

4. Wound.

5. Space of death and resurrection.

6. Hegemonic discourse.

References

Adams, R. (2023, 16 June). Student loan debt in England surpasses £200bn for first time. *The Guardian*. Available at: www.theguard ian.com/education/2023/jun/16/student-loan-debt-in-england-surpasses-200bn-for-first-time [Accessed: December 14th, 2023].

Ahmed, S. (2017). *Living a Feminist Life*. Durham: Duke University Press.

Ahmed, S. (2021). *Complaint!* Durham: Duke University Press.

Al-Khalili, J. (2010). *Pathfinders: The Golden Age of Arabic Science*. London: Penguin Books.

Alarcón, N. (1990). The theoretical subject(s) of This Bridge Called My Back and Anglo-American feminism. In: G. Anzaldúa, ed., *Making Face, Making Soul/Haciendo Caras: Creative and Critical Perspective by Feminists of Color*. San Francisco: Aunt Lute Books, pp. 356–369.

Almeida, W. D. (2019). *Mulher indígena e lei Maria da Penha: uma análise discursiva transdisciplinar para apreender a constituição da subjetividade fronteriza*. PhD dissertation. Universidade Federal de Mato Grosso do Sul.

Alves, M. (2021). *Juntar pedaços*. Rio de Janeiro: Malê.

Amos, V., & Parmar, P. (1984). Charting the Journey and Challenging Imperial Feminism. In Charting the Journey: Writings by Black and Third World Women (pp. 90–120). London: Sheba Feminist Publishers.

Amos, V., and Parmar, P. (1984). Challenging Imperial Feminism. *Feminist Review*, 17, pp. 3–19, doi:10.2307/1395006.

Andrews, K. (2011). *Back to black: Black radicalism and the Supplementary School movement*. PhD dissertation. University of Birmingham.

Anya, C. (2020). *Watching Whiteness at work: An examination into the management of a formal racial harassment grievance at a UK university*. MSc thesis. University of London.

Anzaldúa, G. E. (1987). *Borderlands/La Frontera: The New Mestiza*. San Francisco: Aunt Lute Books.

Anzaldúa, G. (2000). Interviews/Entrevistas. AnaLouise Keating, A. L. (ed.). New York: Routledge.

Anzaldúa, G. E. (2012). *Borderlands/La Frontera: The New Mestiza*. San Francisco: Aunt Lute Books.

Anzaldúa, G. E. (2015). *Light in the Dark/Luz en lo Oscuro: Rewriting Identity, Spirituality, Reality*. Durham, NC: Duke University Press.

Arday, J., & Mirza, H. S. (Eds.). (2018). *Dismantling Race in Higher Education: Racism, Whiteness and Decolonising the Academy*. London: Palgrave Macmillan. https://doi.org/10.1007/978-3-319-60261-5

Bainbridge, A., Formenti, L., and West, L. (2021). Conclusion: An Evolution of Ideas. In: A. Bainbridge, L. Formenti, and L. West, eds., *Discourses, Dialogue and Diversity in Biographical Research: An Ecology of Life and Learning*. Leiden: Brill/Sense, pp. 217–226.

Ball, S. (2013). *Foucault, Power, and Education*. London: Routledge.

Ball, S. J. (2013). *Foucault, Power and Education*. Oxon: Routledge.

Barthes, R. (1975). *The Pleasure of the Text*. Translated by R. Miller. New York: Hill and Wang.

Bassel, L. (2017). *The Politics of Listening: Possibilities and Challenges for Democratic Life*. London: Palgrave Pivot, doi:10.1057/978-1-137-53167-4.

Beatty, J. (2007). Women and invisible identities: Women as the other in organizations. In: D. Bilimoria and S. Piderit, eds., *Handbook on Women in Business and Management*. Cheltenham and Camberley: Edward Elgar, pp. 34–56.

Beavan, K. (2020). Breaking with the masculine reckoning: An open letter to the Critical Management Studies Academy. In: A. Pullen, J. Helin, and N. Harding, eds., *Writing Differently*. Vol. 4, *Dialogues in Critical Management Studies*, pp. 91–112. London: Emerald Publishing.

Berlant, L. (2022). *On the Inconvenience of Other People*. Durham: Duke University Press.

Bhambra, G. K., Gebrial, D., and Nişancıoğlu, K., eds. (2018). *Decolonising the University*. London: Pluto Press. https://s3.amazonaws.com/supadu-imgix/plutopress-uk/pdfs/look-inside/LI-9780745338200.pdf [Accessed: December 14th, 2023]

Bhopal, K. (2018). *White Privilege: The Myth of a Post-Racial Society*. Bristol: Policy Press.
Bloor, M. (2001). Techniques of validation in qualitative research: A critical commentary. In: R. M. Emerson, ed., *Contemporary Field Research: Perspectives and Formulations*. Prospect Heights, IL: Waveland, pp. 383–395.

Blythe, I., and Sellers, S. (2004). *Hélène Cixous: Live Theory*. London and New York: Continuum.

Bolton, P. (2012). *Education: Historical Statistics*. House of Commons Library SN/SG/4252. Available at: https://researchbriefings.files.parliament.uk/documents/SN04252/SN04252.pdf [Accessed 17 July 2024].

Bourdieu, P., and Champagne, P. (1999). Outcasts on the inside. In: P. Parkhurst, S. Ferguson, J. Emanuel, J. Johnson, and S. T. Waryn (Trans.). *The Weight of the World: Social Suffering in Contemporary Society*. Stanford: Stanford University Press, pp. 421–426.

Brah, A. (1996). *Cartographies of Diaspora: Contesting Identities*. London: Routledge.

Britton, J. et al. (2020). *The Impact of Undergraduate Degrees on Lifetime Earnings*. London: The IFS. Available at: https://ifs.org.uk/publications/impact-undergraduate-degrees-lifetime-earnings [Accessed: 17 July 2024].

Brown, T. T. C., & Murray, E. N. (2023). Navigating a womanist caring framework: Centering womanist geographies within social foundations for Black academic survival. In C. J. Porter, V. T. Sulé, & N. N. Croom (Eds.), *Black feminist epistemology, research, and praxis: Narratives in and through the academy*. New York, NY: Routledge.

Bryan, B., Dadzie, S., & Scafe, S. (1985). *The Heart of the Race: Black Women's Lives in Britain*. London: Virago Press.

Burke, P. J., and Dunn, S. (2006). Communicating Science: Exploring Reflexive Pedagogical Approaches. *Teaching in Higher Education*, 11, pp. 219–231.

Burkhard, T. (2022). Facing post-truth conspiracies in the class-room: A Black feminist autoethnography of teaching for libera-tion after the summer of racial reckoning. *Departures in Critical Qualitative Research*, 11(3), 24–39. https://doi.org/10.1525/dcqr.2022.11.3.24

Butcher, J., Fraser, L., Harman, K., and Sperlinger, T. (2017). *Understanding the impact of outreach on access to higher education for adult learners from disadvantaged backgrounds: An institutional response*. The Open University. Available at: www.open.ac.uk/about/wideningparticipation/about/england/access-observat ory/projects/understanding-impact-outreach-adult-learners-disadvantaged [Accessed: December 14th, 2023].

Butler, J. (1990). *Gender Trouble: Feminism and the Subversion of Identity*. New York: Routledge.

Callender, C., and Mason, G. (2017). Does Student Loan Debt Deter Higher Education Participation? New Evidence from England. *Annals of the American Academy of Political and Social Science*, 671, pp. 20–48, doi:10.1177/0002716217696041.

Callender, C., Hawkins, E., Jackson, S., Jamieson, A., Land, H., and Smith, H. (2014). *"Walking tall": A critical assessment of new ways of involving student mothers in higher education*. Nuffield Foundation. Available at: https://www.nuffieldfoundation.org/wp-content/uploads/2019/11/Callender204005220-2020Final20Report20Nuffield20Full20Report20Walking20tall20Dec202014.pdf, [Accessed 4th, December 2023]

Campt, T. (2017). *Listening to Images*. Durham: Duke University Press.

Choak, C. (2022). *Decolonisation and Higher Education: Closing the Degree Awarding Gap*. Open University.

Cixous, H. (1975). Sorties: Out and out: Attacks/ways out/for-ays. In: H. Cixous and C. Clément, *The Newly Born Woman*. London: Tauris, pp. 63–130.

Cixous, H. (1976). Laugh of the Medusa. *Signs*, 4, pp. 875–893.

Clover, D. (2010). A Contemporary Review of Feminist Aesthetic Practices in Selective Adult Education Journals and Conference Proceedings. *Adult Education Quarterly*, 60, pp. 233–248.

Clover, D. E., Harman, K., and Sanford, K., eds. (2022). *Feminism, Adult Education and Creative Possibility: Imaginative Responses*. London: Bloomsbury.

Clover, D. E., Sanford, K., and Butterwick, S., eds. (2014). *Aesthetic Practices and Adult Education*. London: Routledge.

Clover, D., Sanford, K., and Harman, K., eds. (2022). *Feminism, Adult Education and Creative Possibility: Imaginative Responses*. London: Bloomsbury Critical Education.

Colchado, Lea. (2020). *Making face, making soul, making space for chicanas' traumatic narratives: Autohistoria-teoría as method and genre*. MA thesis. Texas State University.

Collins, C., and Cooper, J. (2014). Emotional Intelligence and the Qualitative Researcher. *International Journal of Qualitative Methods*, 13, pp. 88–103.

Collins, P. (1990). *Black Feminist Thought in the Matrix of Domination*.

Collins, P. (2000). *Black Feminist Thought: Knowledge, Consciousness, and the Politics of Empowerment*. New York: Routledge.

Collins, P. H. (1989). The Social Construction of Black Feminist Thought. Special Issue: Common Grounds and Crossroads: Race, Ethnicity and Class in Women's Lives *Signs*, 14(4), pp. 745–773.

Collins, P.H. (2000). *Black Feminist Thought: Knowledge, Consciousness and the Politics of Empowerment*. New York: Routledge.

Collins, P. H. (2000). *Black Feminist Thought: Knowledge, Consciousness, and the Politics of Empowerment*. 2nd ed. New York: Routledge.

Collins, P. H. (2000). *Black Feminist Thought: Knowledge, Consciousness, and the Politics of Empowerment*. 2nd ed. London: Routledge.

Collins, P. H. (2000). *Black Feminist Thought*. London and New York: Routledge.

Collins, P. H. (2019). *Intersectionality as Critical Social Theory*. Durham: Duke University Press. Available at: http://ebook central.proquest.com/lib/bbk/detail.action?docID=5826042 [Accessed: 18 February 2022].

Crenshaw, K. (2014). Kimberle Crenshaw on intersectionality: "I wanted to come up with an everyday metaphor that anyone could use." Available from: http://www.newstatesman.com/lifestyle/2014/04/kimberl-crenshaw-intersectionality-i-wan ted-come-everyday-metaphor-anyone-could   [Accessed   3 December 2023]

Crenshaw, K. W. (1989). *Demarginalizing the Intersection of Race and Sex: A Black Feminist Critique of Antidiscrimination Doctrine, Feminist Theory, and Antiracist Politics*. University of Chicago Legal Forum, 1989(1), 139–167.

Crenshaw, K. W. (2003). Intersectionality and Identity Politics: Learning from Violence against Women of Color. In W. K. Kolmar & F. Bartkowski (Eds.), Feminist Theory: A Reader. Boston, MA: McGraw-Hill, pp. 533–542.

Crenshaw, K. W. (2006). Intersectionality, Identity Politics and Violence against Women of Color. *Kvinder, Køn & Forskning* [Preprint], (2–3), doi:10.7146/kkf.v0i2-3.28090.

Daley, P. (2020). Black women academics: Politics of representation and community activism in the African diaspora. In: J. Etienne, ed., *Communities of Activism: Black Women, Higher Education and the Politics of Representation*. London: UCL, pp. n.d.

Dalrymple, W. (2003). *White Mughals: Love and Betrayal in Eighteenth-Century India*. London: Flamingo.

Denzin, N., and Lincoln, Y. (2005). *The SAGE Handbook of Qualitative Research*. 3rd ed. London: SAGE.

Department of Education and Science. (1965). The organisation of secondary education. Circular 10/65. London: Available at: www.educationengland.org.uk/documents/des/circular10-65.html [Accessed 23 February 2023].

Department of Education and Science. (1987). Higher education – meeting the challenge, Cm 114. Available at: www.education-uk.org/documents/official-papers/1987-wp-higher-education.html#01 [Accessed 2 March 2023].

Dickson, N., and Clover, D. E. (2021). Adult Education, the Arts and Creativity. *Studies in the Education of Adults*, 53(2), pp. 129–132.

Dovey, L., and Awachie, I. (2019). *Decolonising Pedagogy*. [video] SOAS, University of London. Available at: www.youtube.com/watch?v=G2ZSyRpbQTA [Accessed: 31 Jan 2024].

El-Enany, N. (2020). *(B)ordering Britain – Law Race and Empire.* Manchester: Manchester University Press.

Emejulu, A., and Bassel, L. (2020). The Politics of Exhaustion. *City,* 24(1–2), pp. 400–406.

Emejulu, A., and Sobande, F. (2019). *To Exist Is to Resist.* London: Pluto Press.

Emejulu, A., and Sobande, F., eds. (2019). *To Exist Is to Resist: Black Feminism in Europe.* London: Pluto Press.

Enslin, P., and Hedge, N. (2023). Decolonizing Higher Education: The University in the New Age of Empire. *Journal of Philosophy,* 58(2–3), pp 227–241.

Etienne, J. (2016). *Learning in Womanist Ways: Narratives of First-Generation African Caribbean Women.* London: UCL.

Etienne, J. (2016). *Learning in Womanist Ways: Narratives of First-Generation African Caribbean Women.* London: Trentham Books, UCL IOE Press.

Etienne, J. (2020). *Communities of Activism: Black Women, Higher Education and the Politics of Representation.* London: UCL.

Etienne, J. (2022). Imperial College London Series: Belonging – Exploring Our Lived Experiences. Interview with Dr. Jan Etienne. Imperial College London. Available at: https://www.imperial. ac.uk/events/150502/belonging-exploring-our-lived-experien ces-3/ [Accessed 5 December 2023]

Etienne, J., ed. (2020). *Communities of Activism: Black Women, Higher Education, and the Politics of Representation.* London: UCL.

Evans-Winters, V. E. (2019). *Black Feminism in Qualitative Inquiry.* London: Routledge.

Evaristo, C. (2017). *Ocupação Conceição Evaristo.* São Paulo: Itaú Cultural.

Evaristo, C. (2019). *Macabéa: Flor de Mulungu.* São Paulo: Editora Malê.

Fanon, F. (1952). *Peau noire, masques blancs [Black Skin, White Masks].* Paris: Éditions du Seuil.

Foucault, M. (1970). *The Order of Things.* (2nd ed., 2001). London: Routledge.

Foucault, M. (1978). *The History of Sexuality.* New York: Vintage Books.

Foucault, M. (2014). *A Arqueologia do Saber.* Translated by Luiz Felipe B. Neves. Rio de Janeiro: Forense Universitária, 2014.

Freire, P. (1970). *Pedagogy of the Oppressed* (M. B. Ramos, Trans.). New York, NY: Herder and Herder.

Freire, P. (1970). *Pedagogy of the Oppressed.* Ramos, M.B. (Trans.), New York: Herder & Herder.

Georgakopoulou, A. (2015). *Small Stories, Interaction and Identities.* Amsterdam: John Benjamin.

Gibbons, A. (2018). Neoliberalism, Education Policy and the Life of the Academic: A Poetics of Pedagogical Resistance. *Policy Futures in Education,* 16(7), pp. 918–930, doi:10.1177/1478210318774.

Grewal, S. (1992). Home Truths: Stories of Survival and Hope by African and Asian Women. London: Virago.

Griffiths, K. (2013). *Is Anglo-Indian Culture Dying Out?* BBC News. Available at: www.bbc.co.uk/news/magazine-20857969 [Accessed 3 February 2023].

Gristy, C., Letherby, G., and Watkins, R. (2020). Schooling, Selection and Social Mobility over the Last 50 Years: An Exploration through Stories of Lifelong Learning Journeys. *British Journal of Educational Studies,* 68(2), pp. 161–177, doi:10.1080/00071005.2019.1589416.

Guerra, V. M. L. (2017). As fronteiras da exclusão: o discurso do outro e o processo identitário do indígena. In: M. A. Bessa-Oliveira, E. C. Nolasco, V. M. Lescano Guerra, and Z. R. Nolascodos S. Freire, eds. *Fronteiras Platinas em Mato Grosso do Sul (Brasil/Paraguai/Bolívia): biogeografias na arte, crítica biográfica fronteiriça, discurso indígena e literaturas de fronteira.* Campinas: Pontes, pp. 95–122.

Hackman, H. (2005). Five Essential Components for Social Justice Education. *Equity & Excellence in Education*, 38, pp. 103–109.

Hackney Council online. (2022). Child Q, Hackney.gov.uk. Available at: https://education.hackney.gov.uk/content/response-child-q [Accessed 23 June 2024].

Hall, S. (2019). *Essential Essays*. Volume 2, *Identity and Diaspora*. Durham: Duke University Press.

Harney, S., and Moten, F. (2013). *The Undercommons: Fugitive Planning & Black Study*. New York: Minor Compositions.

Harvey, D. (2007). A Brief History of Neoliberalism. Oxford: Oxford University Press.

Haynes, C., Joseph, N. M., and Allen, E. L. (2020). Toward an Understanding of Intersectionality Methodology: A 30 Year Literature Synthesis of Black Women's Experiences in Higher Education. *Review of Educational Research*, 90(6), pp. 251–787.

Haynes, E., Walker, R., Mitchell, A. G., Katzenellenbogen, J., D'Antoine, H., & Bessarab, D. (2021). Decolonizing Indigenous health: Generating a productive dialogue to eliminate Rheumatic Heart Disease in Australia. *Social Science & Medicine, 277*, 113829. https://doi.org/10.1016/j.socscimed.2021.113829

Hayward, B. (2014). *An exploration into the extent to which the gendered legacy of care resides in contemporary "spaces of femininity," with specific reference to the roles the learning support assistant performs*. MSc thesis. Birkbeck College, University of London.

Hayward, B. (2019). *An exploration of the subject positions of the female learning support assistant, as they practise their art and craft in the everyday*. PhD dissertation. Birkbeck College, University of London.

Hayward, B., Hatfield, C., Zsigo, L., & Lane, V. (2022). Habitual Currents, Part 1, and Flying Above and Beyond, Part 2. In B. Hayward (Ed.), *Resilience Embodied in Conversations and Creativity During a COVID Context*. The European Conference on Education 2022: Official Conference Proceedings. Nagoya, Japan: The International Academic Forum, pp. 61–72.

Hedin, E. L. (1934). The Anglo-Indian Community. *American Journal of Sociology*, 40, pp. 165–179.

hooks, b. (1984). *Feminist Theory: From Margin to Centre*. Boston: South End Press.

hooks, b. (1989). *Talking Back: Thinking Feminist, Thinking Black*. London: South End Press.

hooks, b. (1990). Choosing the margin as a space of radical openness. In: *Yearning: Race, Gender, and Cultural Politics*. Toronto: Between the Lines, pp. 15–23

hooks, b. (1994). *Teaching to Transgress: Education as the Practice of Freedom*. London: Routledge.

hooks, b. (1994). *Teaching to Transgress: Education as the Practice of Freedom*.

hooks, b. (1995). *Art on My Mind: Visual Politics*. New York: The New Press.

hooks, b. (1995). Intelectuais negras. *Estudos Feministas, Florianópolis*, 3(2), pp. 464–478. Available at: https://periodicos.ufsc.br/index. php/ref/article/view/16465/15035 [Accessed: 26 July 2023].

hooks, b. (1999). *All About Love: New Visions*. New York: William Morrow.

hooks, b. (2000). *Feminism Is for Everybody: Passionate Politics*. London: Pluto Press.

hooks, b. (2002). *Feminist Theory: From Margin to Center*. Boston, MA: South End Press.

hooks, b. (2003). *Teaching Community: A Pedagogy of Hope*. New York: Routledge.

hooks, b. (2020). *Feminist Theory from Margin to Center*. 2nd ed. London: Pluto Press.

Hoult, E. (2012a). *Adult Learning and La Recherche Féminine: Reading Resilience and Hélène Cixous*. New York: Palgrave Macmillan.

Hoult, E. (2012b). Recognizing and Escaping the Sham: Authority Moves, Truth Claims and the Fiction of Academic Writing about Adult Learning. *InterActions: UCLA Journal of Education and Information Studies*, 8(2), pp. 1-24.

Hoult, E. C. Mort, H., Pahl, K., and Rasool, Z. (2020). Poetry as Method – Trying to See the World Differently. *Research for All*, 4, pp. 87–101.

Hunt, C. (2009). "They pass by themselves without wondering": Using the Self in, and as, Research. In: P. Coare and L. Cecil, eds., *Really Useful Research: Critical Perspectives on Evidence-Based Policy and Practice in Lifelong Learning*. Proceedings of the 39th Annual SCUTREA Conference. Cambridge: University of Cambridge, pp. 255–262.

Jackson, S. (2004). Language and discourse in the academy. In: *Differently Academic?* London: Kluwer Academic Publishers, pp. 101–125.

Jensen, K., and Bennett, L. (2015). Enhancing Teaching and Learning through Dialogue: A Student and Staff Partnership Model. *International Journal for Academic Development*, 1324, pp. 1–13.

Jones, P. (2021). Ghetto Skolar (Struggles) ft. Anonimas. *Spotify*. Available: https://open.spotify.com/track/0cFkWaeF86XT9xk7421SAG?si=5c9a9dfcee0c418b

Jordan, J. (2002). Some of Us Did Not Die: New and Selected Essays. New York: Basic Books.

Jordan, J. (2002). *Some of Us Did Not Die*. New York: Basic Civitas Books.

Kay, J. (1988). The Adoption Papers. Newcastle upon Tyne: Bloodaxe Books.

Keating, AnaLouise (2005). *Entre mundos/Among Worlds: New Perspectives on Gloria Anzaldúa*. New York: Palgrave Macmillan.

Kilomba, G. (2020). *Plantation Memories: Episodes of Everyday Racism*. Münster: UNRAST-Verlag.

Landor, L. (1988). Motherlands: Black Women's Writing from Africa, the Caribbean and South Asia. London: The Women's Press.

Lather, P. (2000). Against Empathy, Voice and Authenticity. *Women, Gender, and Research*, 4, pp. 16–25.

Leavy, P. (2008). *Method Meets Art, Arts-Based Research Practice*. Guilford: Guildford Press.

Lewis, G. (1988). Forming Nation, Framing Welfare: The Politics of Race and Migration in Post-War Britain. London: Routledge.

Lewis, G. (2000). *Race, Gender, Social Welfare: Encounters in a Postcolonial* Society. London: Polity Press.

Lewis, G. (2005). "Feminist Review": 25 Years and Beyond. *Feminist Review*, 81, pp. 5–11. Available at: www.jstor.org/stable/3874336 [Accessed: 18 April 2019].

Lewis, G. (2017). Questions of Presence. *Feminist Review*, 117(1), pp. 1-19.

Lewis, G. (2020). Once More With My Sistren: Black Feminism and the Challenge of Object Use. *Feminist Review*, 126(1), pp. 1–18, doi:10.1177/0141778920944372.

Lindsay-Dennis, L. (2015). Black Feminist-Womanist Research Paradigm: Toward a Culturally Relevant Research Model Focused on African American Girls. *Journal of Black Studies*, 46(5), pp. 506–520. Available at: www.jstor.org/stable/24572888 [Accessed 15 April 2021].

Lorde, A. (1980). Age Race, Class, and Sex: Women Redefining Difference. In: *Sister Outsider*. New York: The Crossing Press, pp. 114–123.

Lorde, A. (1989). *A Burst of Light: Essays*. Ithaca, NY: Firebrand Books.

Lorde, A. (2015). The Master's Tools Will Never Dismantle the Master's House. In: Moraga and G. Anzaldúa (eds.), *This Bridge Called My Back*. 4th ed. Albany: SUNY Press, pp. 94–97.

Lorde, A. (2019). *Sister Outsider*. London: Penguin Random House.

Lugones, M. (2003). *Pilgrimages/Peregrinajes: Theorizing Coalition against Multiple Oppressions*. Lanham: Rowman & Littlefield.

Lugones, M. (2010). Toward a Decolonial Feminism. *Hypatia*, 25(4), 742–759.

Lygo-Baker, S., Kinchin, K., Winstone, N., eds. (2019). *Engaging Student Voices in Higher Education: Diverse Perspectives and Expectation in Partnerships*. London: Palgrave Macmillan.

Macaes, B. (2018). *The Dawn of Eurasia: On the Trail of the New World Order*. New Haven: Yale University Press.

Macaulay, T. B. (1835). *Minute on Indian Education*. Calcutta: British Government of India, p. 1–11.

MacLure, M. (2011). Qualitative Inquiry: Where Are the Ruins? *Qualitative Inquiry*, 10, pp. 997–1005.

Maisuria, A., and Cole, M. (2017). The Neoliberalization of Higher Education in England: An Alternative Is Possible. *Policy Futures in Education*, 15(5), pp. 602–619, doi:10.1177/1478210317719792.

Maitlis, P. (1998). The revolution in England's universities 1980–2000. [Online] Warlight.Tripod.com. Available at: https://warlight.tripod.com/MAITLIS.html#:~:text=Up%20until%20the%20early%201980's,into%20University%20on%20leaving%20school [Accessed 17 July 2023].

Massey, D. (1996). *Space, Place and Gender*. Cambridge: Polity.

Mathibela, N. (2020). And they didn't die: Black women and the silencing of activist voices. In: J. Etienne, ed., *Communities of Activism: Black Women, Higher Education and the Politics of Representation*. London: UCL Institute of Education Press, University College London, pp. n.d.

Maylor, U. (2020). Supporting UK black sisters in UK higher education. In: J. Etienne and Communities of Activism, eds. London: UCL Press, pp. n.d.

Mbembe, A. J. (2016). Decolonizing the University: New Directions. *Arts & Humanities in Higher Education*, 15(1), pp. 29–45, doi:10.1177/1474022215618513.

Metcalf, S. (2017, 18 August). Neoliberalism: The idea that swallowed the world. *The Guardian*. Available at: www.theguardian.com/news/2017/aug/18/neoliberalism-the-idea-that-changed-the-world [Accessed 15 December, 2021].

Mignolo, W. (2012). Decolonizing western epistemology/building decolonial epistemologies. In: A. M. Isasi-Díaz, and E. Mendieta, eds., *Decolonizing Epistemologies: Latina/o Theology and Philosophy*. New York: Fordham University Press, pp. 19–43.

Mignolo, W., and Walsh, C., eds. (2018). *On Decoloniality: Concepts, Analytics, Práxis*. Durham: Duke University Press.

Mirza, H. S. (1997). *Black British Feminism*. London: Routledge.

Mirza, H. S. (2009). Chapter 14: Postcolonial Subjects, Black Feminism, and the Intersectionality of Race and Gender in Higher Education. *Counterpoints* 369, pp. 233–248. Available at: www.jstor.org/stable/42980391 [Accessed 15 April 2021].

Mirza, H. S. (2014). Decolonizing Higher Education: Black Feminism and the Intersectionality of Race and Gender. *Journal of Feminist Scholarship*, 7, 1–12.

Mirza, H. S. (2015). "Harvesting our collective intelligence": Black British feminism in post-race times. *Women's Studies International Forum*, 51, pp. 1–9, doi:10.1016/j.wsif.2015.03.006.

Mirza, H. S. (2018). Decolonizing Higher Education: Black Feminism and the Intersectionality of Race and Gender. *Journal of Feminist Scholarship* 7(Fall), pp. 1–12. Available at: https://digitalcomm ons.uri.edu/jfs/vol7/iss7/3 [Accessed 17 December 2021].

Moffett-Bateau, A. (2015). Feminist erasures: The development of a Black feminist methodological theory. In: K. Silva and K. Mendes, eds., *Feminist Erasures: Challenging Backlash Culture*. London: Palgrave Macmillan UK, pp. 54–71, doi:10.1057/ 9781137454928_4.

Moraga, C., and Anzaldúa, G., eds. (1983). *This Bridge Called My Back: Writings by Radical Women of Colour*. 2nd ed. Boston: Women of Color Press.

Moreno, A. (2005). Superar a exclusão, conquistar a equidade: refor-mas, políticas e capacidades no âmbito social. In: E. Lander, ed., *A colonialidade do saber: eurocentrismo e ciências sociais*. Translated by Júlio Cézar Casarin Barroso Silva. Buenos Aires: CLACSO, pp. 187–202.

Moreton-Robinson, A. (2000). *Talkin' Up to the White Woman: Indigenous Women and Feminism*. Brisbane: University of Queensland Press.

Nash, J. C. (2019). Black Feminism Reimagined: After Intersectionality. Durham, NC: Duke University Press.

Nash, J. C. (2019). *Black Feminism Reimagined: After Intersectionality*. Durham, NC: Duke University Press.

Nayak S. (2015). *Race, Gender and the Activism of Black Feminist Theory*. London: Routledge.

Nayak, S. (2019). *Intersectionality in Social Work: Activism and Practise in Context*. London: Routledge.

Nolasco, E. C. (2004). *Restos de ficção: a criação biográfico-literária de Clarice Lispector*. São Paulo: Annablume.

Nolasco, E. C. (2013). *Perto do coração selbaje da crítica fronteriza*. São Carlos: Pedro & João.

Oakley, A. (1981). Interviewing women: A contradiction in terms. In: H. Roberts, ed., *Doing Feminist Research*. London: Routledge & Kegan Paul, pp. 30–62.

Ohajunwa, C. O., and Mji, G. (2021). Expressing Social Justice within Indigenous Research: A Reflection on Process and Affirmation. *AlterNative: An International Journal of Indigenous Peoples*, 17(2), pp. 183–190.

Obasi, C. (2019). Decolonising the Academy: Towards a Radical Reformation. *The Journal of Critical Education Policy Studies*, 17(2), 245–260.

Olufemi, L. (2020). *Feminism, Interrupted: Disrupting Power*. London: Pluto Press.

Owton, H. (2017). *Doing Poetic Inquiry*. London: Palgrave Macmillan.

Oyewumi, O. (2002). Conceptualizing Gender: The Eurocentric Foundations of Feminist Concepts and the Challenge of African Epistemologies. *Jenda: A Journal of Culture and African Women Studies*, 2(1), pp 1–9. Available at: www.africaknowl edgeproject.org/index.php/jenda/article/view/68 [Accessed 4 December 2023].

Parker, R., and Pollock, G. (1981). *Old Mistresses: Women, Art and Ideology*. London: Pandora Press.

Patterson, A., Kinloch, V., Burkhard, T., Randall, R., & Howard, A. (2016). Black feminist thought as methodology: Examining intergenerational lived experiences of Black women. *Departures in Critical Qualitative Research, 5*(3), 55–76. https://doi.org/10.1525/dcqr.2016.5.3.55

Porter, C. J., Sulé, V. T., & Croom, N. N. (Eds.). (2023). *Black feminist epistemology, research, and praxis: Narratives in and through the academy*. Routledge pp. 271–313.

Puwar, N. (2004). *Space Invader: Race, Gender and Bodies Out of Place*. Oxford: Berg.

Radice, H. (2015). How We Got Here: UK Higher Education under Neoliberalism. *ACME: An International Journal for Critical Geographies*, 12(2), pp. 407–418. Available at: https://acme-journal.org/index.php/acme/article/view/969 [Accessed 5,. December 2023].

Reay, D. (2004). Education and Cultural Capital: The Implications of Changing Trends in Educational Policies. *Cultural Trends*, 20, pp. 73–86.

Reay, D. (2005). Beyond Consciousness? The Psychic Landscape of Social Class. *Sociology*, 39, pp. 911–928.

Reay, D. (2012). What would a socially just education system look like?. *Journal of Education Policy*, 27(5), pp. 587–599. https://doi.org/10.1080/02680939.2012.710015

Reay, D. (2018). *Miseducation: Inequality, Education and the Working Classes*. Bristol: Policy Press.

Reay, D., Crozier, G., and Clayton, J. (2010). "Fitting in" or "Standing out": Working-Class Students in UK Higher Education. *British Educational Research Journal*, 1, pp. 107–124.

Reynolds, T. (2008). Ties that bind: Families, social capital and Caribbean second-generation return migration. [University of Sussex] Working Paper 46.

Richardson, L. (1997). *Fields of Play*. New Brunswick, NJ: Rutgers University Press.

Rigney, L.-I. (1999). Internationalization of an Indigenous Anticolonial Cultural Critique of Research Methodologies: A Guide to Indigenist Research Methodology and Its Principles. *Wicazo Sa Review*, 14(2), pp. 109–121.

Rivera Cusicanqui, S. (2012). Ch'ixinakax utxiwa: A reflection on the practices and discourses of decolonization. *South Atlantic Quarterly*, Winter, pp. 95–109.

Rustin, M. (2016). The Neoliberal University and Its Alternatives. *Soundings*, 63(Summer), pp. 147–170. https://www.lwbooks.co.uk/soundings/63

Santos, B. de S. (2008). *Desobediência epistêmica: a opção descolonial e o significado de identidade em política*. Cadernos de Letras da UFF – Dossiê: Literatura, língua e identidade, no. 34, pp. 287–324.

Santos, B. de S. (2010). Para além do pensamento abissal: das linhas globais a uma ecologia de saberes. In: B. de S. Santos and M. P. Meneses, eds., *Epistemologias do Sul*. Coimbra: G.C., pp. 23–71.

Saunders, P. (2009, October 29). *Poverty of Ambition: Why We Need a New Approach to Tackling Child Poverty* (N. Evans, Ed.). Retrieved from https://www.cps.org.uk/

Scheurich, J. J., and Young, M. D. (1997). Coloring Epistemologies: Are Our Research Epistemologies Racially Biased? *Educational Researcher*, 26(4), pp. 4–16.

Sharpe, C. (2016). *In the Wake: On Blackness and Being*. Durham, NC: Duke University Press.

Singh, J. (2018). *Unthinking Mastery: Dehumanism and Decolonial Entanglements*. Durham: Duke University Press.

Smith, L. T. (1999). *Decolonizing Methodologies: Research and Indigenous Peoples*. London: Zed.

Society of Biology. (2013). *Women in academic STEM careers: A contribution from the Society of Biology to the House of Commons Science and Technology Select Committee.* London: Society of Biology. Available at: www.rsb.org.uk/images/Society_of_Biology_response_to_women_in_STEM_careers_inquiry.pdf [Accessed 20 January 2024].

Solomon, S. J., and Ehlinger, B. (2023). Does Black Lives Matter Support Moderate the Effect of Procedural Justice on Legitimacy? Testing the Procedural Justice Invariance Thesis. *Policing: An International Journal*, 46(4), pp. 639–654.

Spillers, H. J. (1987). Mama's Baby, Papa's Maybe: An American Grammar Book. *Diacritics*, 17(2), pp. 64–81.

Spivak, G. C. (1988). Can the Subaltern Speak? In C. Nelson & L. Grossberg (Eds.), *Marxism and the Interpretation of Culture.* Urbana, IL: University of Illinois Press, pp. 271–313.

Stenhouse, R. (2014). Re/presenting patient experience as poems. *Journal of Psychiatric and Mental Health Nursing*, 21, pp. 423–437, doi:10.1111/jpm.12094.

Stevens, J. (2013). Army of teaching assistants faces the axe as Education Department attempts to save some of the £4 billion they cost each year. *Daily Mail* [online]. Available at: www.dailymail.co.uk/news/article-2334853/ [Accessed 5 March 2015].

Tharoor, S. (2018). *Inglorious Empire: What the British Did to India.* London: Penguin Books.

Torres, S. (2005). La conciencia de la mestiza /towards a new consciousness: uma conversação inter-americana com Gloria Anzaldúa. *Revista Estudos Feministas*, 13(3), 720–737.

Unruly Women. (2022). Nucleus, Halpern Gallery, Kent. 12–25 May 2022.

Vergès, F. (2021). *A Decolonial Feminism.* Translated by Ashley J. Bohrer. London: Pluto Press.

Wahern. (2022). Contemporary Womanist Research Post George Floyd: Compelling Developments in Black Feminist Theory. Birkbeck, University of London.

Walker, A. (1983). *In Search of Our Mothers' Gardens*

Walker, A. (1983). *In Search of Our Mothers' Gardens: Womanist Prose.* San Diego: Harcourt Brace Jovanovich.

Wallace-Sanders, K. (2009). *Mammy: A Century of Race, Gender, and Southern Memory.* Ann Arbor: University of Michigan Press.

Weale, S. (2022, 13 November). Dismay at threat of "devastating" job cuts at Birkbeck, University of London. *The Guardian.* Available at: www.theguardian.com/education/2022/nov/13/dismay-at-threat-of-devastating-job-cuts-at-birkbeck-university-of-london [Accessed 04, June 2024].

Weissman, S. (2024). Administrator's suicide leaves campus reeling with 'despair' and 'disappointment.' *Inside Higher Education.* Available at: https://www.insidehighered.com/news/governance/executive-leadership/2024/01/12/lincoln-university-administrators-suicide-roils, [Accessed 5th, June 2024]

Wenger, E. (1998). *Communities of Practice: Learning, Meaning, and Identity.* Cambridge: Cambridge University Press.

West, L. (2016). *Distress in the City: Racism, Fundamentalism and a Democratic Education.* London: UCL Press.

Williams, D. (1993). *Sisters in the Wilderness: The Challenge of Womanist God-Talk* Maryknoll, NY: Orbis.

Williams, T. (2023, 12 January). How Birkbeck was squeezed by years of neglect for adult education. *Times Higher Education.* Available at: www.timeshighereducation.com/depth/how-birkbeck-was-squeezed-years-neglect-adult-education [Accessed 3 December 2023].

Woolf, V. (1927). *To the Lighthouse.* (New ed., 1994). London: Wordsworth's Classics.

Wright, C. (2005). Chapter 4 "Hello Trouble": Black women academics and the struggle for change. In: J. Etienne, ed., *Communities of Activism: Black Women, Higher Education and the Politics of Representation*. London: UCL Institute of Education Press, University College London.

Wright, C., Maylor, U., & Pickup, T. (2020). Young British African and Caribbean Men Achieving Educational Success: Disrupting Deficit Discourses about Black Male Achievement. London: Routledge

Wynter, S. (1990). Afterword: Beyond Miranda's meanings: Un/Silencing the "demonic ground" of Caliban's woman. In: C. B. Davies and E. S. Fido, eds., *Out of Kumbla: Caribbean Women and Literature*. Trenton, NJ: Africa World Press, pp. 355–372.

Zapate, N. (2018). Making and Unmaking of Anglo-Indian Identity in Late Colonial India. *Proceedings of the Indian History Congress*, 79, pp. 405–411. Available at: www.jstor.org/stable/26906273. [Accessed 3 February 2023].

Recommended further activities

How might Black feminist principles in an ethic of care help to decolonise everyday practice in higher education policy and practice?

How can we understand the ways in which the UK, British higher education sector can learn from globalised Black feminist academic discourse to help decolonise the British higher education academy?

How do we develop strategies for academics to survive in a neoliberal university?

What might a decolonising collaborative programme look like?

Index

www.ingramcontent.com/pod-product-compliance
Lightning Source LLC
Chambersburg PA
CBHW050352270326
41926CB00016B/3714